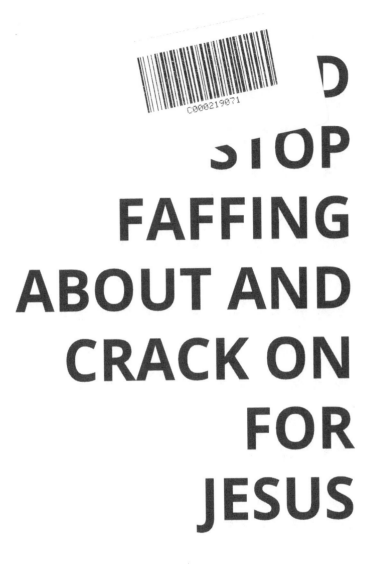

D

STOP
FAFFING
ABOUT AND
CRACK ON
FOR
JESUS

Rowena Cross

Text layout and cover design Helen Jones

Dedicated to Harriet

Acknowledgements

It takes a village.

There are so many people to thank when you write a book. It is never really a solo project.

Jesus. Without you there would be no reason for a book.

Ron, my first and last love.

Bella and Woody, two of the best blessings God ever gave me, I love you so much.

Bear for teaching me what fearless love is and showing me how God loves me.

Lozza and Matt, Rosie and Adam – without you guys we wouldn't know Jesus.

My earthly family, Mum, Dad, Connie, Kirsty, Darcy and Aston.

My friends and prayer warriors:

Loraine, Sonia, Julie CB, Gen, Twinny aka Karen, Amelia, Elaine, Carrie, Jane, Sarah A, Jo, Kathryn and Andy, Vicky, Jacqui L, Wendy and Andrew, Dave P, Stephen G, Rachel Y, Hali and Ben, Bob and Wendy, Amy, Jude and Brenton, Laura and Max, Laura B, Susie M and the company of prophets on both sides of the world whom I love dearly.

Kim Mc, my fellow PW friend, for keeping me sane in LA.

Louie – the best mentor and friend anyone could ever have.

My Tivoli Cove, Malibu, family: Antonia and Scott, Jyl and Beej, Bridget and Christine.

Neal – your prayers were significant in this book's journey, thank you friend.

Bob Goff and his dream big writing team – thank you for inflating my balloon!

Helen and Wendy for seeing the vision and helping me reach it.

And our church families past and present, you have all been the true meaning of the word family to us from the crazy aunt, to the loving mum to the annoying little brother.

St Georges Church, Georgeham, where it all began, and we found him.

St Matthews Church, Bristol, where we trained and let go of the reins.

St Andrews Church, Cullompton, where we learned to love like Jesus and be loved.

St Saviours Church, Sunbury, where we learned to go far out of the boat with Jesus.

Vintage Church, Malibu, where we learned his love really does cross oceans.

I send this book out in the name of JESUS and pray that you will hear His voice speaking to you through it.

What others say:

"This is a God-inspired book to give an injection of faith to his people. Jesus wants to transform every aspect of your life and use you for his glory. This is how Rowena lives her life and it is inspirational. Full of honest, faith-filled stories of following Jesus, with practical principles to apply from lessons she has learned. Read it and go and live the life Jesus is calling you to"

Revd Canon John McGinley
Executive Director, Myriad: multiplying churches in England
New Wine, Head of Church Planting Development

"Reading this was a bit like a ride in a funfair. Entertaining, challenging, encouraging and so faith building. This is a book that will build your faith muscle. Read it and be inspired by God's pursuit of us and a life determined to pursue God."

Rev'd Prebendary Mark Melluish
Senior Pastor
St Paul's Ealing, St John's Ealing & St Mellitus Hanwell

"Rowena Cross is a glorious example of a life transformed by the love & mercy of Jesus. She simply "beams" Jesus in everything she says and everything she does. If you lack courage in an area of your life, then let Ro walk alongside you through the pages of this book (as she has done for so many of us) and let her love, faith, passion, courage and hunger for the things of the Lord bring you hope, encouragement & joy.

This book is infectious, life-transforming and filled with stories of the goodness & mercy of God that will make you laugh, and a few that will make you cry. But every chapter will bring you closer to the path the Father has set before you. Read it and be transformed."

Fergus Scarfe
Regional Director
GOD TV

"Rowena is a full-on lover of Jesus and is deeply passionate about Christians being mobilised to spread the Gospel. Her story is compelling and her message urgent. This is a book for today and a catalyst to seeing the Body of Christ fulfill her commission!"

Ric (Bishop of Islington) & Louie Thorpe

"There's no faffing about in Rowena's story. Right from the first page, it's a whirlwind journey through her life, involving crises, discovery, failure, humour, friendship, faith, pain, purpose, questions, honesty, tears and coming to terms with what really matters this side of heaven. Rowena wears her heart on her sleeve and faces reality head on, deeply rooted in her encounter with someone called Jesus who she'd love you to meet. As you'll read, if you're not dead yet, this book is for you!"

David Taviner
Director of Broadcasting UCB

BE BOLD STOP FAFFING ABOUT AND CRACK ON FOR JESUS

Contents

Then he said to me, "Speak a prophetic message to these bones and say, 'Dry bones, listen to the word of the Lord! This is what the Sovereign Lord says: 'Look! I am going to put breath into you and make you live again! I will put flesh and muscles on you and cover you with skin. I will put breath into you, and you will come to life. Then you will know that I am the Lord.'"

So, I spoke this message, just as he told me. Suddenly as I spoke, there was a rattling noise all across the valley. The bones of each body came together and attached themselves as complete skeletons. Then as I watched, muscles and flesh formed over the bones. Then skin formed to cover their bodies, but they still had no breath in them.

Then he said to me, "Speak a prophetic message to the winds, son of man. Speak a prophetic message and say, 'This is what the Sovereign Lord says: Come, O breath, from the four winds! Breathe into these dead bodies so they may live again.'"

So, I spoke the message as he commanded me, and breath came into their bodies. They all came to life and stood up on their feet—a great army.

Ezekiel 37:4-10

1 from coma to life

At about 4am on a cold Sunday morning in January 2002, I was awoken by a sharp kick to my back, and I was shaking from head to toe. I still believe the unborn daughter in my tummy woke me up to tell me we were in trouble. I was thirty-nine weeks pregnant. We went to hospital, and they found I had a fever. Or, in the very British words of the midwife as she ripped my T-shirt off, 'You are a little bit toasty'. So, they gave me paracetamol to bring the fever down and called for the doctor and anaesthetist urgently. The anaesthetist was huge. When he arrived, he seemed to fill the room with his presence. I remember thinking how joy-filled he was, and I felt safer now he was there. He then gave me an epidural and a doctor gave me penicillin at the same time. He warned me that as I had low blood pressure, I may feel a bit weird. Both drugs pumped into my body and that is when it went horribly wrong. I said to him, 'I feel weird, something's wrong.' He looked at me and said, 'That is not the weird I meant.'

My body started to convulse, and they started to panic. My husband froze at the end of the bed with his hand covering his mouth, so I knew I looked bad. I had suffered a major allergic reaction to one of the drugs they had given me. I couldn't breathe or speak but I could see and hear everything. It was terrifying. I remember looking into the eyes of all the mask-wearing people who had rushed into the room and seeing fear. One of the doctors tried to get me to sign a consent form and I remember thinking 'what are you doing, you silly woman – I can't even breathe, let alone write.' The worst part was when they asked my poor husband who they should save, me or our unborn daughter. That question haunted me for weeks afterwards. They rushed me out of the room and left Ron on his own. I was now in another room with even more people rushing about. I felt afraid. No one was speaking to me; they were just rushing around me. All of a sudden, a peace came over me as I realised that in a minute, it would stop. This awful dying feeling would stop. One way or another. They would fix me, or I would die. Either way, that thought brought me peace for the first time. Maybe God spoke to me in that moment without me knowing. The last thing I remember before going into unconsciousness is the sound of a very cheap, plastic, Bic type hair razor scraping across my skin – so my last words before going unconscious were: 'I bet I will pay for that later.' I mean, seriously, could I not have said something more profound? People asked me afterwards, 'What was your last thought?' 'Did you see a light?' Embarrassingly, I had to explain that my last thought was about annoying stubble rash!

I was now in a coma.

My husband was told that I wouldn't survive and if I did survive, I would be in a vegetative state. Our daughter was taken out quickly in an emergency caesarean as her heart rate had dropped, and she was taken to a special care unit. I was being kept alive by a machine. My mum and dad quite recently had started attending a church and, when my husband rang them, they asked their church to pray. My mum said she didn't know who was on the phone as he was so distressed. But she realised it was Ron and it was bad. After that call Ron got down on his knees and prayed for the first time. He said, 'If you are there God, now is the time to show up. I will do anything if you save my wife.'

At that moment when he prayed and the church prayed, I opened my eyes. I had been in a coma for only four hours, but it felt like four years to Ron. I was in intensive care in a room on my own with my own individual, specialist nurse and the blinds were drawn. It's somewhere they don't expect you to return from. But I was awake. The nurse watching over me jumped as I spoke. My community midwife was holding my hand, crying. I was confused but still understood that it was unusual for her to be there. She told me when she got the call, she repeated all the way to the hospital, 'Please don't let it be Rowena, please don't let it be Rowena', because she knew how afraid I was beforehand. Ron and our families were allowed in, and they all cried. I didn't - I was in deep shock, fear and pain. I was also very confused. I would go to say a sentence and the wrong word would come out. I felt like a shell of a person watching what was happening from far away. It was bizarre; the doctors kept coming in and telling me repeatedly that it was a miracle. Asking me if I understood it was a miracle. But I didn't at that moment. Because I didn't know what a miracle was. I had never been to church, read the Bible or even met a Christian, so the word 'miracle' meant nothing to me!

I remember they moved me in the middle of the night, but I still needed specialist care, so they put me in the labour ward as it was staffed twenty-four hours a day. It was the worst night of my life. I was so traumatised and left all alone listening to women screaming as they gave birth. I asked for a TV just so I could try and drown out the noise. I didn't sleep all night. My family and some friends came to see me the next day, but I was consumed by fear and couldn't share it with them. It was day two and the hospital then moved me to the normal maternity ward and put me in a public ward with four other women. I asked if I could have a private room but was told no.

That night I stayed awake again as I was in pain and shock and wouldn't let them give me any drugs. I cried when they made Ron go home. I was now left alone with the very people, the medical professionals, who, before all of this, I trusted and felt safe with. Only now I felt completely afraid of them. I remember a nurse telling me off for being awake. The memory of this still makes me cry as I type it eighteen years later. But I couldn't sleep. I had no pain relief as they didn't know what I was allergic to so I wouldn't let them give me any. I just had paracetamol and some form of ibuprofen. My hands were black and swollen from where the doctor had tried to find a vein whilst I was dying so I couldn't sit myself up properly without help. So, I just lay there – scared, alone and in pain.

The next day I was so weak my husband had to hold me up in the shower. Finally, someone took my blood and realised how much blood I had lost and said I had to have a transfusion. Something inside me broke and I started screaming: 'Get away from me, get away from me. You have already tried to kill me once.'

Suddenly a private room was found (funny that!).

Apparently, I was scaring the other women. That is not what I saw. What I saw was a ward full of new mums looking at me with love and compassion. I was so traumatised I had a breakdown. I discharged myself from hospital on day three, shaking from head to toe. I will always remember our lovely GP turning up at our home after we arrived and telling us he was signing Ron off for six weeks as we needed time together to heal – a kind act that helped us start the long journey to healing. And so began a horrific journey back to health – just me, Ron and our beautiful baby, Isabella. Not only was I a miracle – Bella was too. She was completely unharmed and as Mary Poppins says, 'Perfect in every way.'

So, the three of us ran away and bought a bed and breakfast hotel hundreds of miles away in Yorkshire. I think we were trying to get as far away from the pain as possible. The problem is you take the pain with you and are now hundreds of miles away from your family and friends. We clung to each other and our wonderful gift of a daughter who was a complete joy. All the while I was having very intense therapy to deal with the trauma and depression. Seeing the therapist was the worst time of my week. He would sit my chair in the middle of the room, and he would sit behind a desk and just stare at me and wait for me to speak. It was horribly traumatic revisiting things and then he would just stop me and say: 'Times up – see you next week.' I would leave crying and bewildered not knowing what to do with my feelings until the following week. It is an inhumane way to treat people and I am glad they no longer use that method in the UK. Writing this and revisiting that place to remember the details, I realise how dark it really was. At that point there was no Jesus, no knowledge of God, no loving church, just man-made philosophies to try and help me make sense of what had just happened. I have since had another round of therapy and it was completely different. Even in the darkest of times, the light was still on. I was never in complete darkness again. Even when the light was so faint it was barely visible, it was on, none the less. I had never realised that before and wanted to share it with you. Maybe it will bring you hope too.

A couple of years on, around the beginning of 2004, we moved to Devon. Isabella had developed baby asthma and our lovely GP in Yorkshire had said she would thrive better by the sea. Can you imagine a GP saying that today? I have often wondered if he was a Christian. So, bizarrely, we sold our business and moved to Devon in the southern end of

England. We were driving through a lovely village called Georgeham and Ron heard a voice say: 'You have to buy that place', as we drove past a shop and B&B! He then did the boy thing and made me ring them and ask if they would sell it to us, as it wasn't actually for sale. The voice on the other end of the phone gave me many reasons why they wouldn't like to do that. I then heard a voice whisper to me, 'Leave your number', so weirdly I did. People ask us if it was weird hearing the voice – but the weirdest thing was, it wasn't weird! Someone rang us back twenty minutes later and asked how we knew they were thinking of selling. We told them we didn't. Six months of process and paperwork later, we moved in and what God had done (without us knowing him) was place us at the heart of a very active Christian community.

We were very open about why we were there and how much pain we were still in some days. We were running the village shop. It was the heart of the village in that you saw and talked to almost every person that lived there every single day. We knew who was sad, poorly, grieving or alone. We had the pleasure of celebrating in people's joy too. When we arrived, there was a waiting list for therapy in Barnstaple, so they assigned me a psychiatric nurse in the meantime. For some reason his job title filled me with embarrassment and shame. What was worse is that he had to walk through the shop to get into our house. I shared my worry that people would recognise him, and I will never forget what he said. 'Rowena, if they know who I am then they, too, may have been where you are. I am sure they, more than anyone, will understand how hard it is to do what you are doing.' I will always remember how encouraging he was. My favourite line he said was in reference to the awful chair-in-the-middle-of-the-room therapy I had in Yorkshire. He said: 'You got

1 from coma to life

better in spite of that man NOT because of him.' (He also called him a word I can't print in a Christian book.) I don't know why but I found this comment strangely encouraging.

We noticed straight away that some of the people who befriended us were different. We described them as having a light inside them that the rest of the world didn't have. We were drawn to them uncontrollably. They showed us love and friendship but didn't seem to want anything from us. Being from London (and in advertising, which, quite frankly, at that time was up there with estate agency for swimming with sharks) there were times when it felt like people were only nice to me when I was useful to them. You know when they want something. These people were different. They told us about Jesus. They say they didn't, but that *we* bombarded *them* with questions. But, whatever, they told us about Jesus and his love for us.

2 finding Jesus

One morning we woke up and said we wanted to go to church. God is super organised, as it was a Sunday. Imagine if it had been a Tuesday and a painting group or something had been there. But it wasn't; it was a Sunday so off we went. Our friends almost pole-vaulted over the pews to stop us meeting 'that' member of the congregation. If you don't know who 'that' member of the congregation is, then maybe it's you. Just saying. We had no idea what was happening. We just stood up when they stood up and sat down when they sat down. But we did spend the whole service in floods of tears in this small rural church by the sea. It was kind of like an out-of-body experience. But we described it as 'like we had come home'. To what, we had no idea, but we knew we had 'come home'.

The church put on an Alpha course, pretty much just for us, and there we found out more about Jesus and his love. At the end we decided to give it a go – this Christian thing and we jumped in headfirst and said, 'Yes,' to Jesus. Well, if we are keeping it real, what actually happened was that we didn't have a babysitter for Alpha, so we kind of alternated weeks, so I missed most of it and had to do it again. So, at the end of my SECOND Alpha course, I went home and said to Ron, 'We are in.'

And Ron in his normal laid-back way said, 'Yes dear. I was in weeks ago, but I was waiting for you to be in too.'

So cool, but also slightly annoying. At the end of the course I remember bombarding Duncan, the Baptist Minister with questions like, 'How can I be a Christian? I am too naughty.'

He said: 'Ro, faith is not something you bolt on to your existing life. It must become the centre *of* your life from which everything else flows.'

It was powerful, the truth, and has stuck with me ever since. We were discipled and loved so well by that lovely, little church by the sea. We started hosting a variety of things in the village and would tell anyone who would listen that Jesus loved them. We were on fire with his love.

The Vicar, Brian, was very clever. He got us to host a house group and he led it. I felt a bit like a small child in a class full of adults most of the time, but I loved being able to ask questions and get answers. I remember Brian's lovely, kind wife Eunice telling me in her gentle, Irish accent to, 'Learn to rest in the Psalms, Ro.' It was gentle and good advice. We also started to invite around fifty people from the village who didn't know Jesus into our house every month for a bring and share lunch. We hoped they would come to church and find Jesus too. We thought this was what you did when you were a Christian. We didn't really know what a bring and share lunch was. In fact, we did have someone phone and ask us, 'What kind of *chair* would you like me to bring?'

* * *

We weren't alone in not understanding 'Christianese' as I called it. But we wanted people like us to know about Jesus and what he was doing for us. I remember wondering if anyone would ever give their life to Jesus, come to church or understand his love until at one lunch I stopped in the middle of the chaos and looked around. I realised it was 5pm; the house was still bursting with people, laughing and chatting together. Someone was emptying my dishwasher, someone else was vacuuming my floor and all the children were on the trampoline or in the pool. Jesus' love in action. Nobody wanted to leave his presence. They were discovering just like we did that when you find Jesus, you find community – family – too. But you see, up until we moved to that village in Devon aged thirty-four, no one had shared the gospel with us. No one had invited us to church. We would actually say, up until that point, we had never met a Christian, which is, of course, a big fat lie.

The hard truth of it, actually, was that, up until that point, we were not valuable enough to be told the good news. Christian people looked at us and said our NO for us. But we NEEDED the gospel, we SEARCHED for it, but it was just that no one had shared it with us. The church needs to wake up and hear that. So, if you are reading this and haven't heard it yet – here it is just for you, my darling. Jesus loves YOU. He is relentlessly pursuing a relationship with you. You are NOT your circumstances; you are NOT what you have done or what has been done to you. You are a beautiful child of God, and he is waiting for you with open arms. I wanted to tell you that in case you had never heard it previously. You see, I promised Jesus that I would spend the rest of my life telling people how he loves them.

3 headstand at the post office

In around 2009/2010 we left that village we called home (with many tears) for my husband to start training as a Church of England vicar (that is a pastor or priest if you are not from the UK). Me – the wife of a vicar? Are you joking, Lord?! Have you not heard what comes out of my mouth? It is important to say that this, quite rightly, didn't happen overnight. Ron went through an eighteen-month discernment process before we left. It's intense especially for someone who identifies as a new Christian. My husband described the process as turning him inside out. But what was miraculous about the process was that at no point did anyone comment that he hadn't been a Christian long enough. His call was clear.

* * *

This is a good point to pause here and note that depth of faith is not correlative to length of faith. How long we have been a Christian is not a demonstration of how deep our faith is. There are people who would have identified themselves as Christians for years who have only ever attended church once a month and dipped in and out of their Bibles. Equally, there are people who don't believe they are 'real' Christians yet as they are so new, but have given their life to Jesus, read their Bibles every day and are in church whenever it is open, hungry to be involved. Which one is a Christian? Phew – well thank the Lord that we don't decide that. God does.

As it says in 1 Samuel 16:7:

'The Lord does not look at the things people look at. People look at the outward appearance, but the Lord looks at the heart.'

I think that is why God let someone so inexperienced (to human eyes) like me set up a ministry during Ron's curacy (more about that later). I am a learn-on-the-job kind of person. And I would love to tell you that we sailed off into the sunset to Bristol and it was all amazing. But that would be a lie. It was so hard. Suddenly we had been thrust into a world I didn't understand. I watched from what felt like afar as Ron's face lit up each day as he went off to college and immersed himself in all things Jesus. It was truly inspiring to watch. But it was a very different experience for me. I was like a fish out of water and still felt I had more in common with the mums at the school gate than the Christians at Ron's college. I was also still travelling to London to work once or twice a week, so that didn't help as we were having very different experiences.

An example was, they had this group at Ron's college called, Connect, for the spouses, to help us meet people in the same situation as us and help us settle in. Well, I have never felt less connected to anything in my whole life. I felt like I had been dropped onto a different planet, one where I didn't speak the language and had no idea what was happening.

Now before you think I am being mean about these wonderful people, let it be stated for the record I am completely aware that this was mainly all my stuff, not theirs; well, almost all my stuff! So, I didn't go very often. The most wonderful thing I got from Connect were my darling friends Gen, Laura and Twinny (who was actually called Karen but it's what she named us as we were very similar). One day as I was sitting amongst the group, feeling like that kid in Charlie Brown's class (you know, dirty blanket and flies around me) I was suddenly alerted to the following story.

A lady was praying for a whole month and every day she heard God say the same thing: 'Go and do a headstand outside the post office.' What? She prayed every day and all she heard was, 'Go and do a headstand outside the post office.' My ears pricked up like antenna. After a month of this she got so fed up that she said: 'Fine, Lord. Today I will go and do a headstand outside the post office.' At this point I was thinking are you quite mad woman? Have you forgotten we are British and not in the Olympic gymnastics team? Just as she was about to do the headstand a man shouted at her 'STOP!' She turned round and asked him why. This is the exchange that followed:

Man: 'What are you doing?'

(Me in my head: Don't say doing a headstand outside the post office....)

Woman: 'Doing a headstand outside the post office.'

Man: 'Why?'

(Me in my head: Don't say God told you, don't say God......)

Woman: 'Because God told me to when I prayed.'

(Me in my head: Wow there you go he is going to think you are completely mad now!)

Man: 'But you couldn't have known. How did you know? My life is *so* bad that I said to God today I am going to end it all. And if you are really there, God, if you exist you will give me a sign and make someone do a headstand outside the post office today.'

Wow. Silence.

Just let that sink in.

That story blew my mind, and I was changed forever by it – the beauty of God being in the whole of that situation. Firstly, God knew the woman intimately. It's a beautiful demonstration of how God knows us and loves us. He knew her well enough to know how long he needed to give her the oddest of instructions before she would obey. He trusted her with that prayer knowing she would obey him. Me – I would maybe have needed about seventy more years, a pillow and some serious antibacterial gel before I would have considered it! But that woman – just a month. Secondly, God knew when the man who didn't know him yet would come to the end of his coping. He was involved with the man way before the man was involved with him. He loved the man in advance of the man loving him back. And as only God can he caused those two worlds to collide to save a soul.

But at the same time what I am thankful for and started to learn whilst in Bristol is where my heart was for Jesus. You see, God often speaks the loudest to us in our most painful and disorientating times. More accurately, I wonder if the truth really is that it is in those times, we pay most attention to his voice? Anyway, this story stuck deeply in my soul because God was helping me understand that I had a deep compassion for the lost, a compassion he had placed there as he knitted me together in my mother's womb. I understood how the mums at the gate felt much more than I could relate to the mums at the Christian college because that is how HE made me. That was a God-given compassion. There in Bristol God started that realisation in me of my calling.

In the headstand story a faithful woman of prayer saved the life of a lost soul that day in more ways than one. And by that faithful lady recounting that story at the Connect group another 'just found' soul at the beginning of their journey with Jesus (me in case that wasn't clear), had a big seed of encouragement planted in her. That is the God we worship, and he deserves the whole of us not just a Sunday two-hour part. Or the bit we have left over at the end of the week. The whole of ourselves. Jesus died on the cross so we could be his hands and feet on earth whilst forgiven and saved. He is calling us to be a reflection of him. That deserves all of ourselves, every day of our lives in service to him.

Will you take up the challenge? Maybe stop for a minute and ask God what seed he is planting in you through this story? Can you feel your heart stirring? What is that and what does it mean? Sit quietly and wait for him to reveal it to you. Put on some worship music and sing and see what comes into your mind from him as you worship him. Then write it down somewhere – somewhere you can look back on it in the future, where he WILL reveal that seed has turned to fruit.

You see, Jesus doesn't look at us and see our mistakes or our shortcomings – oh no. He looks at us and sees our potential. He sees us as we really are. Not how the world sees us, or indeed how we see ourselves. He is always there with us. We turn away from him (or are never told about him or aware of him in the first place), not the other way round. So, for those of us who are not paying attention (me? Never!) he has to find us in a more radical way – he uses our pain. I love the description of pain given by C. S. Lewis:

'It is God's megaphone to rouse a deaf world.' [1]

Never a truer word has been spoken about our world – inattentive sleepy spirits. Ron and I were completely deaf. But in our deepest and most debilitating pain God reached in and saved my life. Not just physically – that was the easy bit. No, he spiritually saved my life and took it from a temporary

---

1 C. S. Lewis on the Problem of Pain, Sunday 08/12/2012 - 22:05, by Jana Harmon, C.S. Lewis Institute (cslewisinstitute.org), p9

and plastic life to an eternal one to be spent with him. What a gift. And I will be forever thankful that God used my pain for his good. And I will serve him for the rest of my days in thankfulness to him and our friends who took a leap of faith and shared his love with us. You are valuable to him. That is why I am writing this book. It is time for you to wake up and rise up into the calling God has for you in this season, TODAY. If I can write a book – then you can do anything.

4 tepid

I cannot bear the state of the Western church right now or the steady sliding away from God that 'Christians' appear to be undertaking. My heart is breaking. Frank Bartleman who wrote an eyewitness account of the 1906 Los Angeles, Azusa Street revival in his book said:

'It is one thing for the church to be in the world, but when the world gets into the church a spiritual decline has set in.' [2]

Wow – how true that is! He said that over one hundred years ago and what has changed? The slow seep of worldly culture into our church is still happening. Like a creeping invisible poisonous fog. Have you seen the film from 1980 called *The Fog*? [3] It is about a slow-moving, terrifying fog filled with dead people that creeps up on people and kills them. Nice! Well, that is what I think is spiritually happening to our churches. But it doesn't need to. I think God is calling his church back to holiness – churches full of Holy Spirit filled, Bible-dependant, on fire, light bearers for Jesus. Our world would look like a very different place if we answered His call with a resounding YES. I am speaking as a former dead person wandering in the aforementioned fog. A former deeply broken person whose soul was crying out for Jesus but didn't know it. And I just know you are part of the solution.

1 Peter 2:9 puts it like this:

'But you are not like that, for you are a chosen people. You are royal priests, a holy nation, God's very own possession. As a result, you can show others the goodness of God, for he called you out of the darkness into his wonderful light.'

---

2 Frank Bartleman, *Asuza Street*, (Whitaker House 1982), p44
3 The Fog (AVCO Embassy Pictures, EDI, Debra Hill Productions, 1980)

BE BOLD STOP FAFFING ABOUT AND CRACK ON FOR JESUS

How exquisite – this is who we REALLY are. As followers of Jesus that is where we start from today. And we can show others the goodness of God because we have been called out of the darkness into his wonderful light. Ask yourself right now these challenging questions. Is that what I look like? Is that what I behave like? Is that what I undertake for Jesus?

I think it is only possible to do or be any of these things if you know who you are in God yourself and operate as a whole-life disciple not a half-in consumer. We go part of the way to answer our previous question of why we don't allow God to work through us if we look at the Bible book of Revelation. This book was written by John and as the name suggests it was a revelation he received from God. And Revelation is both a book of hope but also a book of warning. Things were not as they should have been in churches, so Christ called the members to commit themselves to live in righteousness. But what does that look like?

It seems not much has changed since the Bible was written. Revelation 2 and 3 are more relevant to us today than we might think. One of the things I find inspiring and mind-blowing about the messages to the churches in Revelation is that God wrote to each church individually – speaking intimately into their individual problems – showing how well he knew them – that is actually so loving. It also ultimately shows us NOW that he knows us too. It's a very convicting point for us, isn't it? What would God say about you and your church right now? Because God's plan for us as a church, a body of people, is for us to reach the potential he has set for us. And like all loving fathers he starts with encouragement – by commending where the church once was.

'I know all the things you do. I have seen your hard work and your patient endurance. I know you don't tolerate evil people.

You have examined the claims of those who say they are apostles but are not. You have discovered they are liars. You have patiently suffered for me without quitting.' (Revelation 2:2-3)

Standing out, hard work, low tolerance for evil, being different, not quitting, patient suffering, calling out stuff against Jesus – boom. Sounds like normal expectations for a church, right? But how many of our churches actually display those characteristics? Are they bold enough to go against the flow of the world? Ephesus (one of the churches he wrote to) was also a culture known for its widespread immoral sexual practices and sin. Jesus' words acknowledge that despite great opposition the church in Ephesus had once stood firm against such things. Jesus is acknowledging in that verse that a) its hard and b) its unusual. The more I read Revelation, the more I think it is just describing today! We are also living in these times of widespread sin and sexual immorality. However, just like Ephesus, I think the church today has made excuses and lowered the standards of what the Bible calls us to maintain. The world now calls the sin 'personal choices' or 'alternative lifestyles'. And I fear that once again the church may have subtly (or in some cases massively) agreed!

When the body of believers begins to tolerate sin in the church (which is what we do when we change the Bible, lower our expectations etc.) we choose the world over Christ and we compromise the church's witness. Why don't you ask yourself a question – and answer it honestly – Whose approval do you want? Whose approval do you value the most? God's or the world? And it is OK to admit the world because knowing where you stand is the first step to changing it. As a former people-pleaser and control freak (that is a fun combo) if you had asked me that question a few years ago I couldn't always truthfully say – God. I hated people disliking me or disapproving of me, and that drove me to make some poor decisions and trust all the wrong people. I would work so hard to be liked which is dangerous as not only does it unwittingly give people power over you (never a good thing or a God thing) it is also impossible to achieve. It doesn't leave room for the fact that the humans you are trying to please are well ... human, which means they too, like you, don't have all the answers and make mistakes.

Last year whilst praying I heard these words: 'The spirit of lukewarmity is what is going to kill off our churches if we do not change.'

It is part of the reason I wrote this book. I believe this is a word for now. And. as always, I believe that God has given us the answer in His Word. Let's take a look at the third chapter of Revelation. The book of Revelation really is our last chance to hear what Jesus is saying to us. He loves us SO much that we are warned again and again in the Bible what is really important to us in this world. Ironically, it isn't this world; it is the next one, our eternal life. Let's not beat around the bush – in Revelation 3 he is calling out the lukewarmity in the church. He was saying to the church in Laodicea that unless they changed, he would spit them out. And I think that is the same reason why we aren't on fire for God now too. Lukewarmity. My Bible commentary describes lukewarmity as tasteless and repugnant! It says:

'The believers didn't stand for anything. Indifference had led to idleness. By neglecting to do anything for Christ the church had become hardened and self-satisfied like the world around it. And there is nothing more disgusting than a half-hearted, nominal Christian who is self-sufficient.'

Wow that is direct and full on. Although the language is strong the condition is not final – hurrah! He calls them to repent and turn to him with joy. I think the most profound part of Revelation 3 is this:

'You say, "I am rich. I have everything I want. I don't need a thing!" And you don't realize that you are wretched and miserable and poor and blind and naked. So, I advise you to buy gold from me — gold that has been purified by fire. Then you will be rich.'

Jesus is pointing to our value and time being taken up by all the wrong things. He says you think you are rich, because this world – our culture – values and celebrates monetary success and celebrities and the Laodiceans were no different back then. They were wealthy and self-sufficient and didn't think they needed God either. Nothing has changed. The world still values monetary success – God doesn't. It has no value to him and if you read the stories of celebrities, you will see why. They often say when they were trying to be successful, they thought that when they got there, they would be happy, only to discover it wasn't true. They were then the same person with problems but just with more money. In 2015 Justin Bieber was quoted in *Billboard Magazine* as saying: 'I was close to letting fame completely destroy me'. [4]Praise God he has now found Jesus and is putting his life back together and finally finding out who he is and whose he is. Jesus is speaking into this phenomenon when he says you think you have gold, but you haven't – you don't realise that actually you are wretched and miserable, poor, blind and naked. I know that I have felt like that – some days I still do. And maybe you have felt like that too? Maybe you are right in it at this exact moment. But Jesus offers the solution in the very next sentence. He claims boldly that it is not who you are or who you are meant to be and directs us back to him.

---

4 *Billboard Magazine,* Justin Bieber quote (2015)

There is always a way home to him when we repent and turn towards him.

He says in Revelation 3:18:

'So, I advise you to buy gold from me—gold that has been purified by fire. Then you will be rich.'

Not the riches of the world but his riches. And they are SO different. In fact, having riches in Jesus often looks like failure to our culture – but it isn't, it SO isn't – riches in Jesus are SO, SO good. Apart from anything else they direct your eyes above your circumstances to the truth of his Word – which in turn keeps you from becoming lukewarm. That is why it is so important to read his Word every day. He also tells us to put on his purity and his ointment so we will have his demeanour and his eyes and not the eyes of the world. That way you will really SEE people and the world as he does. There is no way you can remain lukewarm if you have his eyes. It is such a spirit led thing to do; people look so different when you do this.

When I was looking through the quotes of celebrities whose lives had fallen apart (there were loads by the way), I found there were quite a few celebrities who had changed their entire lives and professions after finding Jesus, saying their old lives just didn't fit in with their new life in Jesus. Have you done this? I know that is a challenge God is calling me to every day and it is super hard. Jesus isn't having a pop at us either; no, he quite clearly says in verse 19: 'I correct and discipline everyone I love.' He is demonstrating his love for us – only a loving father would chase after us time and time again full of love and forgiveness. He then calls us to turn from our indifference. And that is what we have, isn't it – indifference. Because we think we have everything we need, don't we? Our success is ours – we earned our money; we did it, didn't we? Absolutely not. As his disciples everything good we have is given to us by him. If you are going to take all the credit yourself for the successes in your life, then you can't blame Jesus when things in your life go wrong in your life too, right?

The wonderful film *God's Not Dead* tackles this in a brilliant debate between a Christian student and an atheist teacher. The teacher says he doesn't believe in God and challenges the student to prove why he believes in God, all the while mocking him in the process. As they get to the climax of the debate the student asks his teacher 'Why do you hate God?' After lots of denying the teacher screams at him 'Because he took everything away from me.' The boy's response is so powerful; he simply says, 'How can you hate someone who doesn't exist?'

If his teacher says God doesn't exist, then there is no one or nothing for him to blame for the things that have happened in your life (bad and good). Pick a lane. There is no middle ground.

And I think we have to do the same. We have to pick a lane. We are either for Jesus or we are against him. There is no middle ground. Jesus himself said this in Matthew 12:30:

'Anyone who isn't with me opposes me, and anyone who isn't working with me is actually working against me.'

That is a powerful statement. The first time I heard it I was struck to the core with it. And I think the church has tried to create a middle ground in the misguided attempt to make Christianity 'more appealing' to the world. But that has backfired. Not only does it not work but it inadvertently created a generation of lukewarm Christians trying to live somewhere in the middle. You are either for Jesus or against him. You see, the gospel doesn't need to be made more appealing. When I heard it for the first time it was the most beautiful thing I had ever heard. Jesus speaking in Matthew gives us some equally challenging words – but they give a huge insight as to where the problem of lukewarmity lies. It lies in our hearts.

In Matthew 23 he refers to the leaders as hypocrites and likens them to whitewashed tombs – perfect looking on the outside but filled on the inside with dead people's bones and all sorts of impurity. Sounds a bit like Instagram, doesn't it? On the outside, to the world we look all shiny and perfect but, on the inside, we are still following our sinful or worldly ways. So, what does lukewarm look like? I think it looks like being half in for Jesus, doing faith on our terms, not reading the Bible every day, turning up when we feel like it, fitting Jesus in around our busy lives, consuming church, not serving, and wanting Jesus to follow us and not the other way round. The irony that God revealed to me whilst I was preparing this chapter was that all the ways we have just listed that look like being lukewarm are actually also the CAUSES of being lukewarm.

And nothing lukewarm is good, is it? Think about it; no one ever said, 'Do you know what – I would love a lukewarm bath right now.' Or 'Who wants a cup of lukewarm tea or coffee?' Or 'Please do give me your lukewarm argument in closing this case, defence lawyer.' Just think of the word, lukewarm – tepid. Tepid, even the word is annoying. I think our politicians have become the perfect demonstration of lukewarmness. I am not sure they stand for anything anymore (except attacking each other in the pursuit of power). They just change their mind at the drop of a tweet. The, quite frankly, enemy-run social media has only made this worse.

So, what does the life of an on-fire disciple look like? To a Christian it means being led by the Holy Spirit in all things, dying to self daily and serving him with your whole heart. Ask yourself – how often do you see those values displayed on social media? Every day we make choices. And at the bottom of those choices, do I want to please God or the world?

You can't choose both. They are actually completely opposed.

The world chooses serving of self over serving others. The world chooses political view over biblical view. The world chooses what they feel over the truth of God's Word.

Which do you choose and how do we change if we want to choose to please the world? I believe change starts with us discussing the problem, not avoiding it and sticking to the more palatable stuff. Now some translations call the Revelation verse I quoted from earlier the 'loveless church', probably because of this line in verse 4 and 5 which should break our hearts as we read them:

'You don't love me or each other as you did at first! Look how far you have fallen!'

Wow – that is so sad. That is Jesus speaking. 'You don't love me as you did at first.' And that is what happens if we remove Jesus from every aspect of society. We lose the greatest demonstration of love the world has ever known. We lose our example. Do you remember your first steps of your Christian life? I can remember mine – you know where you may have had enthusiasm without knowledge. Another great question to ask yourself today is: do I now have knowledge without enthusiasm? Both are necessary if we are to keep our love for God intense, reverent and untarnished by the world. We live in a cancel culture; if it offends me – cancel it. How sad is that? I saw Pastor Craig Groeschel post this great quote on his Instagram account: 'If you are on a continuous search to be offended, you will always find what you are looking for.' [5](A mic drop or a boom emoji should follow that quote.)

We HAVE to ask ourselves how long it will be before someone tries to cancel Christianity. Sound ridiculous? But you need to know it is already happening. In some countries it's overt, oppressive and dangerous which, just as it did with the murder of Stephen in the Bible, has bred fearless, brave Christians who literally die for their faith – they refuse to join the world. If you don't believe me, check out the organisation Open Doors. Their whole reason for existing is to support their persecuted brothers and sisters around the world. Did you know according to Open Doors' world watch list on their website (www.opendoorsuk.org), last year (2021) over 5,000 Christian churches were attacked for their faith? Even more horrifically 5,898 Christians were killed for their faith. It is heartbreaking and I wonder if it is not too harsh to say it is an insult to them for us to be lukewarm. If you want to get involved, then please support them. In fact, it's so important stop reading, visit their website and donate and commit to pray right now.

At the other end of the scale, if you look in the UK, the US and a large proportion of the West, the enemy is in the subtle. It masquerades as being 'inclusive' yet excludes anyone that does not hold and celebrate the same view as the world says it should. As I write this book, I have just read about a pastor in the UK who was thrown out of a hotel mid-conference. Why? – Because his conference was on the value of marriage. Thankfully a group of faithful Christian lawyers didn't just accept this as a 'difference of opinion.' They fought for him, and the hotel apologised publicly. Praise God!

---

5 Craig Groeschel, Instagram (January 2021) P49

5 pigeons learn faster

I was reading recently in the book of 1 Kings in the Old Testament about all the kings and it struck me how similar we are to them. I think God is very clear in how he desires us to be as leaders and whole-life disciples. But as I read about king after king turning away from God and going their own way, I thought to myself, seriously, pigeons learn faster than us humans it seems. Pigeons are actually very intelligent birds according to https://www.pigeoncontrolresourcecentre.org; they were used in the war to deliver post because they were more reliable than humans. So perhaps my analogy is unfair to pigeons!

Anyway, what I am referring to is that one good king followed God with his whole heart and got rid of all the pagan altars and God was pleased, and peace reigned.

The next king would come in and say, 'You know what? I see what you did there and how well that went but, hey-ho, let's bring back the pagan stuff and do it that way.' Everything then went horribly wrong – you know death/destruction etc. ... then the next king served God with their whole heart ... you see where I am going.

That is not even to mention that having kings was not God's choice in the first place. His choice was to have judges – men and women of God who followed him faithfully and judged events on earth through the lens of biblical law not man-made ones. But anyhow, the people demanded kings so, after Samuel, he gave them kings. And they couldn't even get that right, which was why God wanted judges and not kings in the first place, one may argue!

The problem was the kings had no biblical values. Instead of calling on God they relied on self. They followed the people's voices and the power and, well, we have already discussed how dangerous that is haven't we?

For us to know what God has for us and succeed in it we need to learn to hear his voice above the voices of the world; like it says in John 10:14-16:

'I am the good shepherd; I know my own sheep, and they know me, just as my Father knows me and I know the Father. So, I sacrifice my life for the sheep. I have other sheep, too, that are not in this sheepfold. I must bring them also. They will listen to my voice, and there will be one flock with one shepherd.'

I love that Bible verse. Read it again and again until you accept that truth deep down in your heart: Important to note too that God's voice is often a whisper. It is a whisper because he is standing right next to you; he doesn't need to shout. So, how do we really learn to hear his voice and follow his call? Sadly, there is no quick app where we can download it all into our brain quickly. We have to work at it – read our Bible, pray and most of all serve him. It's called spiritual discipline. Not words we talk about much, but they are so important. The practice of getting closer to God every day (through reading his Word, praying and serving) will enrich your life more than you can ever imagine. It's what prevents us becoming lukewarm. When you go into ministry (which is what we are all in for Jesus) it becomes ESSENTIAL to your survival. But it will be your lifeboat. It will be your daily bread. Remember Ephesians 6:12-13:

'For we are not fighting against flesh-and-blood enemies, but against evil rulers and authorities of the unseen world,

against mighty powers in this dark world, and against evil spirits in the heavenly places.

Therefore, put on every piece of God's armour so you will be able to resist the enemy in the time of evil. Then after the battle you will still be standing firm.'

Feeding your soul with God is essential – putting on the armour of God each and every day. And don't confuse nice deeds with serving him. Doing what you are called to do in his name is serving him. The gospel is the greatest message we can give someone and is as relevant today as it was when it was first spoken. The bottom line is, if we are not working for him, then what are we doing and why are we doing it? It is a great question to ask yourself. Do you know we are awake 126 hours a week? Give or take babies and insomnia. How many of those do you currently give to God? That is a hard question, isn't it? Because you see as Pastor Ivery White said in his book *Growing from Convert to Disciple,* 'Jesus isn't looking for cheerleaders. He is seeking men and women who will follow him whatever the cost. He is looking for radical devotion, unreasonable commitment and undivided dedication. Jesus isn't looking for converts. He is looking for disciples.'[6]

Let's throw in at this point another quick tricky question – If you were on trial for being a Christian right now would there be enough evidence to convict you? Woah, I LOVE this question; it challenges me every time! Think about that as you go about life in the next few days. If you were on trial for being a Christian, would there be enough evidence to convict you? So, if all of this is true then what is stopping us being the person he created us to be? Why won't we allow God to work through us for his kingdom?

6 Pastor Ivery White, *Growing from Convert to Disciple,* p8 2019

Why don't you sit now and quietly ask the Holy Spirit to show you any blockages that may be getting in the way of following God. When you hear what they are just ask him to take them away and fill you afresh with his Spirit of Truth. Ask him how *he* sees you and what *he* has for you. Then write down what you hear and keep revisiting it to see how much of what he told you has happened. It is a really encouraging exercise to do.

6 holding the coats

I love the story of Stephen in the Bible. I haven't heard many talks about him, but I find his story so profound. His story starts in Acts 6 with the killer line, 'But as the believers rapidly multiplied there were rumblings of discontent.' Sound familiar? Moaning, us? Never. We never moan, do we? So, they called a PCC or elders meeting of types and appointed seven men who were 'well respected and ... full of the Spirit and wisdom.' Perfect. Stephen was one of those men chosen. He is described as a man of faith and full of the Holy Spirit. I would love it if that was how people described me, wouldn't you? This allowed the apostles to keep teaching the gospel and these men took care of the immediate needs of the people. This plan worked as the next line says, 'So God's message continued to spread.' I love this. The Bible commentary describes this for us as:

'The word of God spread like the ripples on a pond where, from a single centre, each wave touches the next spreading wider and farther. The Good News still spreads this way today. You don't have to change the world single-handedly; it is enough to just be part of that wave, touching those around you.'

YES, let you and me be part of that wave! What a wonderful vision and picture. That is what Stephen, and the other six men, did. They didn't say, 'Oh I want to preach like the apostles; that's way more important.' No, they used their gifts, the wisdom God had given them and the leading of the Holy Spirit to serve in their own way, and this helped the gospel to continue to spread. It says that Stephen performed many amazing miracles and signs among the people. But

BE BOLD STOP FAFFING ABOUT AND CRACK ON FOR JESUS

this attracted the attention of the religious leaders from the synagogue. Instead of rejoicing at the miracles they tried to out debate him to discredit him. But they couldn't. Verse 10 says: *'none of them could stand against the wisdom and the spirit with which Stephen spoke.'*

We need to look at why they needed these six men in the first place to answer the question of why the religious leaders behaved this way. Long before the violent persecution of Christians broke out there was social ostracism. Jewish people who accepted Jesus as the Messiah were usually cut off from their families. So, this care and support of the believers was needed. They depended on each other for support as they were ostracised from the world. This supply of food, homes and resources was a mark of the early church. When the debating tactic hadn't worked to discredit him, they resorted to telling lies about him. But Stephen, despite all this happening, bravely addressed the council of religious leaders from the synagogue. Check out Acts 7 for the brave challenges he spoke of. Suffice to say he didn't hold back from God's truth. He said the unpopular but loving truth so that some might be saved. And that is our job too. We too are to be like Stephen for the sake of the lost and hurting.

This is what happened next:

'But Stephen full of the Holy Spirit, gazed steadily into heaven and saw the glory of God, and he saw Jesus standing in the place of honour at God's right hand. And he told them, "Look I see the heavens opened and the Son of Man standing in the place of honour at God's right hand!"' (Acts 7:55-56)

What was their response to that cry of truth? Verse 57 tells us: *'Then they put their hands over their ears and began shouting.'*

At best that reaction could be observed as really childish. But it's actually, quite frankly, demonic. They put their hands over their ears and began shouting. Think about that carefully now. They were witnessing a man in the presence of God and that was their reaction. If ever we needed to know we are in a spiritual battle between good and evil there is an example right here. They then dragged him out of the city and stoned him.

I prayed with a lovely lady in a jewellery shop as she gave her life to Jesus. God had prompted me to go into the shop and get a charm on my bracelet taken off. I had had the bracelet since I was sixteen and had just rediscovered it. On it was a star sign charm and I felt uncomfortable with it on there. So, I decided I would go to a jeweller and have it taken off and replace it with a cross. The lady asked me why I was having it taken off, so I told her. And that led to a conversation about Jesus which led to her giving her life to him.

I went back a few days later with a Bible gift for her and her boss was there. I immediately sensed the atmosphere had changed as I walked through the door, so I quietly slid the Bible to her and explained it was a gift. She asked her boss if they had any crosses and he looked and said no. He then asked me about my faith, and we got into a discussion. Halfway through me answering one of his questions, he got up and walked across the room to the door. I said something like 'Oh I'm sorry do you have to go somewhere?' and he said, 'NO you do!' I was stunned for a minute as I computed what was really happening. The lady looked mortified and kind of mouthed 'sorry' at me. And I left. I don't believe that man even understood why he had asked me to leave so abruptly in the middle of a perfectly calm conversation. But I did, and it's a mild version of what we are talking about here. He couldn't cover his ears and shout at me (or stone me for that matter) so he did the next thing available to him – ushered me out of his sight. This kind of thing happens to us when we step out for Jesus. I'm not going to pretend it was enjoyable I did sit in my car and shed a tear. But it is a reality. My Ron says to be encouraged when things like this happen. He always says to me 'the light is too bright for some people yet.' It is such a lovely way to look at it. And stories like Stephen encourage me onwards too.

When I reread Acts 7 to write this chapter, a small line pierced my soul as I read it:

'His accusers took off their coats and laid them at the feet of a young man named Saul' (verse 58).

Wait, what? Saul held the coats. Saul who becomes Paul, one of the greatest evangelists for the gospel, held the coats. Did he join in the stoning – no. But he held the coats. This cuts me to my core. How many times do we hold the coats in our lives whilst evil prevails? Nothing in the Bible is there by accident. God wants us to hear the detail. Saul held the coats. When? Just before his road to Damascus moment.

Let's digress briefly and take social media as an example. Over recent months I have seen media (both mainstream and social) get more and more like stone throwing. I have seen that as the political climate heats up so do people's comments. I have seen Christians say vile things about Trump, Biden, Boris Johnson and Jeremy Corbyn. Now we don't KNOW any of these people. These human beings were made in God's image whether they know it yet or not. Where is the disagreement in love? Where are the Christians stepping outside their political choice and bringing the gospel truth into these debates, like Stephen dared to do? I was attacked on Facebook for my beliefs once with some really painful and hurtful words about me in retaliation against my Christian views. I got many (very kind) private messages from Christians saying they supported me but what use is a private message at that time? Where were the public stories of God's very real love in their lives? Fear prevented most people 'getting involved'. They stood by and held the coats, saying nothing.

And don't get me wrong. I am not saying you have to be 'nice' to everyone on Twitter. Stephen certainly wasn't 'nice' by the world's standards in his speech. No, it means deeply loving the people enough to point them to the truth, knowing that in doing so it may make you unpopular with some in the world. It means speaking out when maybe no one else will. We may not be killed for our opinions like Stephen, but people may let us know they don't want to hear the truth and try to silence us in other ways (like they did with me).

But it is our duty; no, it's actually a command from God to keep honouring him with our words and our actions every single day of our lives here on earth. Saying nothing when someone is being bullied, or you see someone spreading lies about God or his church, is like Saul holding the coats. It is not the loving thing to 'not get involved'. We were born and created to get involved and to be different, radically different. If not you, then who? If you need further evidence of why it is so important then the end of Stephen's story is it. Because the end of his story is not just the beginning of the gospel being taken further, it's also the beginning of Saul's story of becoming Paul. You may know already that because of Stephen's death the Christians scattered, and the gospel spread further than it may have done without it. Thank you, Lord.

But perhaps more profoundly was the potential effect it had on the coat-holding Saul, who watched Stephen die whilst he said nothing. Who knows what seed was planted in him seeing Stephen drop to his knees and pray: 'Lord Jesus receive my spirit,' and then shouting, 'Lord don't charge them with this sin.' Stephen's last words as he was murdered were words of mercy for his murderers. What did those words do to Saul? What do they do to you now reading this book? Do they stir your soul with compassion, rage at the injustice or are you indifferent?

I would love to say Saul wandered off and immediately changed his ways. But as with us, Saul was human, and it took another radical move of God a few pages along to really perform that transformation. In fact, the Bible says Saul was 'uttering threats with every breath and was eager to kill the Lord's followers' (Acts 9:1). But God didn't give up on him and neither should we. Just because we don't see with our own eyes the change in someone happening immediately because of our words doesn't mean it isn't happening.

Our job is just to love them and share our story with them and to live out our love and life with Jesus as Stephen did, not just attend church when life is easy. It's to display the radical, life-changing truth of the good news in our actions and choices every day. Saul was God's chosen instrument to bring the gospel. He had a wonderful encounter with Jesus and his life was changed forever. But how many faith-filled seeds were planted in him along the way by faithful followers of Jesus? So, I ask you, do you want to be a coat-holder like Saul or a faithful disciple no matter what the circumstances, like Stephen and Paul?

You can speak up like Stephen, and the many disciples who followed on from him, trusting that the Holy Spirit will give you the right words and the courage and power that you need. God can and will give you everything you need. The amazing thing about Paul is that he was such an unlikely person – it seems impossible that Saul would become Paul. But nothing is impossible with God and that is the beauty of both these stories, and it will be the beauty of your story too if you trust in the Word of God and follow the Holy Spirit in all you do from this day forth.

Why not take a moment now in silence and seek God and all he has to say to you. Then maybe pray the following prayer. It is the covenant spoken by the Methodist movement each year as they recommit themselves to serving God. I love it as it is bold and courageous – why not stop and pray this now.

'I am no longer my own but yours. Put me to what you will, rank me with whom you will; put me to doing, put me to suffering; let me be employed for you, or laid aside for you, exalted for you, or brought low for you; let me be full, let me be empty, let me have all things, let me have nothing: I freely and wholeheartedly yield all things to your pleasure and disposal. And now, glorious and blessed God, Father, Son and Holy Spirit, you are mine and I am yours. So be it. And the covenant now made on earth, let it be ratified in heaven.'[7]

7 Methodist Covenant Prayer, (Methodist.org.uk)

7 halloween and yoga

Let's go deeper into what lukewarmity can look like in our daily lives. Here are two examples of compromise, worldview over biblical view one might say, that can lead to lukewarmity or worse!

Let's start with Halloween. Halloween is huge in the US. I have just returned from two years living in California where my husband replanted a wonderful church. One of my biggest surprises when I moved there was that Christians celebrated halloween. You may not know this, but Halloween celebrates darkness – it is actively following and calling upon the dead and dark forces. When at any other time would we dress up and celebrate that? Also, when else would we tell our children: 'You know we tell you not to speak to strangers and accept candy – well on this one day of the year we are going to knock on doors and do exactly that!' I know that around the world it is seen as a culturally acceptable thing to do but that doesn't make it right for us as Christians, as ambassadors for Jesus.

The man who leads the 'church of Satan' (yes, apparently there is one and I refuse to point you to his website so this quote will remain unreferenced) allegedly said, 'I'm glad that Christian parents let their children worship the devil at least one night out of the year.' If he said that, then that quote chills me to the depths of my soul.

I also want to share with you that I haven't always known this about Halloween. Before I knew Jesus, we dressed up our eldest as a witch with her cousin as something equally hideous and took a photo of them. That photo really troubles me now. At the time I was ignorant to what I was 'harmlessly celebrating'. We found Jesus the next year and we didn't celebrate it anymore. Interestingly, no-one told us we couldn't or shouldn't; it just jarred powerfully within our souls with what we had just learned about the love of Jesus. So as a couple we decided we wouldn't partake in it anymore. That has meant some interesting and difficult discussions with friends (and our children) over the years particularly ones who have, in kindness, invited our children to join in their celebrations. Thankfully as we are involved in church leadership, we were able to put on alternatives like light parties, celebrating the light of Jesus, and firework nights in our garden for the community. Even if we did cause a hoo-ha with our giant bonfire that freaked out our neighbours and meant suddenly the fire brigade became part of our firework celebrations!

But again, like other things, it's about our heart. Do we look different to the world if we join in with the worldly culture of Halloween? The Bible says the world looks at the outer appearance, but God looks at our hearts. And what if celebrating halloween (even if we leave out the bits we feel are dodgy and too far) gives a little piece of our heart to the devil or pours a little drip of water on our Holy Spirit fire thus turning it lukewarm. Think about it: if we do that for too long before we know it our fire will be completely out. Do you want to risk that? By the way, it's never too late to change even if you have been celebrating it all your life – I am living testimony to that. How powerful would that be to your family and friends watching around you if you suddenly said no to halloween?

The second example really shows how the enemy is in the subtle: yoga. When I went to California, I realised that this is a big thing there too. But again, what surprises me the most is how many Christians think yoga is harmless to do.

I realise that this is controversial to say out loud but it's important that we talk about and face the difficult questions to truly grow in our walk with God and win the battle. Yoga is a good example of how we can slide quite inadvertently into lukewarmity without intending to. Did you know that yoga is a Hindu spiritual and ascetic discipline – a spiritual discipline that Hindus practice as part of their faith? Did you also know if we say the word 'namaste' we are bowing to a Hindu god? No, I didn't either until I researched yoga. The Bible is quite clear what God thinks of us worshipping other gods; it doesn't end well. But it's a great example of the world taking something from a faith (you know, pick-and-mix style) repackaging it and owning it for itself. Just by saying 'I don't do it as part of a faith; I do it for stretching and health', does not make it a fact.

It is a bit like a child holding out his hand filled with chocolate at dinner time and saying: 'Mum I'm going to eat this now.' When the mum says 'chocolate is not good for you right before dinner' the kid replies, 'Oh no mum. This isn't chocolate; this is actually vegetables. I have decided it is vegetables and have renamed it so that makes it vegetables.' It's a silly analogy but you get my point. And this example isn't to shame people who do yoga, but it is to challenge the reality of what the world is actually doing and why – before we join in.

As only God can do, an example popped up on my newsfeed in such God-ordained timing. It was the news in a national newspaper of a church that was being widely berated (with even a call for the prime minister to intervene). What on earth did they do that the prime minister needed to get involved, we all wonder? Did they sacrifice animals on the altar? Burn the Bible? No, they turned down a yoga teacher when she requested to use their church hall for her yoga classes. They said their hall was 'made to be used for activities which are compatible with the Christian faith.' Which as it is a church hall sounds fair enough to me. But apparently not. What got me most upon reading this story were two things. The first was the comment from the denominational body itself which really demonstrates the point I am making about it being a slippery slope. Their spokesperson said:

'Each parish is independent and can set its own policies for letting a church hall. Many parishes are entirely open to hosting yoga exercise classes, emphasising the health benefits for both individuals and communities which yoga offers.

'Some parishes feel that because yoga has its spiritual roots in Hinduism and Buddhism, it does not fit with Christian spirituality which is rooted in the love of God revealed in Jesus; and so, they do not allow traditional yoga classes, but would welcome other health and fitness groups such as Pilates.'

This response feels as weak willed as Pilate at Jesus' trial. It effectively throws the church leader under the bus whilst reminding everyone that some churches will allow yoga. It panders to a worldview rather than lovingly saying we follow Jesus, and he has asked us not to worship other idols as it hurts us in the long run. But he loves you too, so come and find out about that love.

The second thing that got to me was that in the yoga teacher's argument of utter disgust at being refused the space, they used the fact that another local vicar was ATTENDING the yoga class as an example of why it can't be all that bad and why this particular hall is just out of date. Yes, that is right – you heard me correctly. Another church leader from a different church was attending the class. I mean I don't even have the words (how rare!) ... it's a slippery slope.

The big potholes of the enemy are easy to spot like murder, being unfaithful to your husband or wife, stealing etc. We all agree those are not what God has for us, right? The Ten Commandments are clear and understood by most Christians. In fact, even the world agrees in the most part that these things aren't good. But just like with Halloween, it is in the subtle where the enemy takes ground in our hearts because it's well ... subtle, and not always easy to spot.

So, let me ask you, how is your heart today? What does God see when he looks at your heart? Because God wants our whole heart. Not just the bits we are happy to hand over. He wants all of it – all of us – good and bad. Isaiah 29:13 says:

'And so, the Lord says, "These people say they are mine. They honour me with their lips, but their hearts are far from me. And their worship of me is nothing but man-made rules learned by rote."' '

All through the Old Testament the prophets predicted how we, as a people, would continue to withhold our whole selves – our hearts – from God. Maybe we would turn up and go through the motions but never believe that his love is actually for us and as a result would become lukewarm in our praise, lukewarm in our reading, lukewarm in our service and lukewarm in our love of Jesus. Then in the New Testament God uses people like Paul to warn the church:

'You should know this, Timothy, that in the last days there will be very difficult times. For people will love only themselves and their money. They will be boastful and proud, scoffing at God, disobedient to their parents, and ungrateful. They will consider nothing sacred. They will be unloving and unforgiving; they will slander others and have no self-control. They will be cruel and hate what is good. They will betray their friends, be reckless, be puffed up with pride, and love pleasure rather than God. They will act religious, but they will reject the power that could make them godly. Stay away from people like that.' (2 Timothy 3:1-5)

What if some of the stuff we do in our lives that we think is harmless is really actually harmful? What if 'stuff' like this is actually stealing our souls and getting in the way of the One who will HEAL our souls. I think that gives us another great question to ask right now, doesn't it? When we are not sure we can ask God 'Will this steal or heal my soul, Lord?' It's a subtle difference but leaves no room for the slippery slope – because it is a slippery slope. Sticking the word Christian in front of something doesn't make it Christian. Let's try it: Christian Hinduism, Christian atheism or Christian pole dancing! Oh, Ro, you are making such a fuss about nothing; it's just a bit of yoga. There is no harm in it.

Really?

What if, when we turn around, the millimetre where we stepped off the line has suddenly become a mile and we have totally lost sight of the path? That is another way we become lukewarm. We get lost. The further we move from the source of the love – JESUS – the harder it is to hear or reach.

I know if I miss a day's Bible study, I find it so much harder to start again the next day. The only way for me to stay on the path is to do it every day, no matter what – which is hard and requires sacrifice of other things.

And trying to stay part of the world's world view is a dangerous thing anyway. The world doesn't even know what its view IS anymore because it changes SO often based on social media. The only way to remain on fire is to stay close to the source of the fire – Jesus. He tells us to start with repenting, which means we have to acknowledge that it is happening and that we are sorry. And that is not about condemnation of the body of Christ but conviction as the body of Christ. It absolutely IS possible for us to accept and love all people AND refuse to tolerate any evil. God cannot tolerate sin and he expects us to stand against it and stand for his truth. The world NEEDS Christians like that.

So, if what you have just read about Halloween, or yoga has resonated with you and your life right now, then you can choose to pray the prayer below. I chose to pray a prayer like this about Halloween and many other things when I became a Christian (and at other times since as I go deeper with God), so you are not alone in this. Maybe there is something else that you are doing in your life that is creating a gap or an idol in your relationship with God. Here is a prayer for you to pray in the quiet of your own home. Remember, repentance, although sometimes sounding quite appropriately like a scary word, means saying sorry to God and vowing to try and not repeat the behaviour. We have the beauty and privilege of knowing when we do this that Jesus went before us and died so we could be forgiven. We know that when we repent, he hears us and responds. Repeat the words and know it's done:

'Lord Jesus, I'm tired of the sin struggle in my life. I feel distant from you. My choices have not led me into the right places. I've listened to the whispers of my enemy instead of your words in Scripture, and the result has been disastrous.

I once walked with you, my heart tender to your leading. Yet little by little, I exchanged your truths for temptations and deceit that led me away from you. Instead of taking thoughts captive and confessing them immediately, I allowed them to grow totally out of control. Repentance was not in my vocabulary. Blame, cover-ups, or trying to reason and rationalise sin never work. They only give birth to deeper sin entanglements.

You created me in your own image, Lord. You know my thoughts before I speak them. You X-ray my heart and see through my excuses and intentions. Your Spirit warned me, but I ignored you. Disappointment and discouragement have taken their toll on me.

So today I'm confessing my desperate need for you. You have promised that if we confess our sin, you will forgive us and make us clean again. Lord, I truly need your forgiveness. Repentance is on my heart and lips. I want to turn around and head in another direction –back to You, Lord. But I need your help.

Just as you created the world out of nothing, Lord, create a clean heart out of my "nothingness". You paid for my sin with your own death. Restore my life and the fellowship we once shared together. You don't condemn me, and you won't disown me; I am your child forever. But I take all the blame – I own my own sin. I am the one who broke fellowship with you and am crushed over the way I treated you and your name.

Lord, root out the darkness and light up my life with your holy presence. Help me understand what went wrong. Show me how my destructive patterns first began. What did I allow to become more important than loving and honouring you? Why did I seek satisfaction in others or other things than you? You are the only one who provides all my needs. You fill up the soul with deep-down joy and peace beyond all understanding.

Lord, may your restoration include new boundaries around my life. I can't flirt with sin and not be hurt. In restoring me, teach me how to say no again to things which could harm me or my testimony. If my actions have wounded others, show me where and to whom I need to ask forgiveness or how to make amends. Help me to surround myself with positive encouragers who will hold me accountable and who will speak the truth in love. Truly, shame melts away and we are healed when we confess to others and ask for their help.

I understand that my repentance won't eliminate the consequences of my sin. Knowing that you don't hold our sins to our account – you remember them no more – and that you place them as far as the east is from the west both humbles me and fills me with amazement and gratitude. No consequence could ever be as painful as knowing how my sin hurt you or how you suffered for me out of love. Your crucifying death gave me eternal life with you. Lord, you place grace next to my regrets and give me hope for a new future.

Thank you, Lord, that sin does not disqualify us. Instead, like a runner who has fallen but who gets up again, I, too, am willing to start again and finish the race you have set for me.

With your restoration, Lord, perhaps I can help others find their way back to you again. I will not give my enemy the victory. Instead, I will accept yours. Instead of a meltdown, with your help I will allow your Spirit to give me a hot heart for you, one that seeks you and wants to live for you the rest of my life. Thank You, Jesus, for your sweet forgiveness and promised restoration.'

Amen.

8 reliant robin or reliance on God?

As a society we rely on a lot of things, don't we? A lot of the time our reliance isn't on Jesus so most of the time those things don't help us at all. Do you remember those Reliant Robin cars? They looked so cool with their three wheels. Del Boy's bright yellow Reliant Robin from British iconic programme *Only Fools and Horses* is probably the most famous one of all time. But they were also famously known for not being very reliable at all, which is ironic considering their name.

So, what does the Bible say about reliance? It says we are to rely on God, and God alone, for everything we need. Some of my favourite people in the Bible who lived out reliance on God were Shadrach, Meshack and Abednego (or your shack, my shack and a bungalow as some people call them). King Nebuchadnezzar, who was possibly a narcissist, built a 90ft statue to himself (nice small ego there). He then demanded that people bow down and worship it (humble!). Well, Daniel's three friends were having none of it. And at the exact moment when King Neb said he would throw them in a boiling hot furnace if they didn't worship his statue, they said these powerful words in Daniel 3:16-27:

"'King Nebuchadnezzar, we do not need to defend ourselves before you in this matter. If we are thrown into the blazing furnace, the God we serve is able to deliver us from it, and he will deliver us from Your Majesty's hand. But even if he does not, we want you to know, Your Majesty, that we will not serve your gods or worship the image of gold you have set up."

Then Nebuchadnezzar was furious with Shadrach, Meshach and Abednego, and his attitude towards them changed. He ordered the furnace to be heated seven times hotter than usual and commanded some of the strongest soldiers in his army to tie up Shadrach, Meshach and Abednego and throw them into the blazing furnace. So, these men, wearing their robes, trousers, turbans and other clothes, were bound and thrown into the blazing furnace. The king's command was so urgent and the furnace so hot that the flames of the fire killed the soldiers who took up Shadrach, Meshach and Abednego, and these three men, firmly tied, fell into the blazing furnace.

Then King Nebuchadnezzar leaped to his feet in amazement and asked his advisers "Weren't there three men that we tied up and threw into the fire?"

They replied, "Certainly, You're Majesty."

He said, "Look! I see four men walking around in the fire, unbound and unharmed, and the fourth looks like a son of the gods."

Nebuchadnezzar then approached the opening of the blazing furnace and shouted, "Shadrach, Meshach and Abednego, servants of the Most High God, come out! Come here!"

So, Shadrach, Meshach and Abednego came out of the fire, and the satraps, prefects, governors and royal advisers crowded around them. They saw that the fire had not harmed their bodies, nor was a hair of their heads singed; their robes were not scorched, and there was no smell of fire on them.' (NIV)

There was no smell of fire on them. Just pause and think for a moment. They were about to be thrown into a furnace so hot that it killed the soldiers who were holding them and STILL they wouldn't deny God and worship this weirdo. Now THAT is trust and reliance on God. I think the most powerful thing they say in this passage is 'but even if he doesn't'. I have got that verse in a frame in my house for inspiration, 'but even if he doesn't'.

Imagine how afraid they must have been, but still they said they would rather die than worship the king's fake god and a 90ft statue: 'We WILL NOT dis our loving Father.' They had trust that God would save them but were prepared to die even if God didn't save them. Now that is reliance on God. What I find really striking about this passage is that their love and commitment to God isn't based on their chosen outcome. It wasn't based on what God might do for them. Their love was unconditional, brave and courageous. And do you know what happened because of their faith and reliance? King Neb (that very same nutter with the statue) then made a decree across the land that EVERYONE must follow the God of Shadrach, Meshach and Abednego. The world they lived in changed because of their reliance on God. I love that – God used the man's very ego to turn a nation around.

What would it look like in your family or community if you were reliant on God as those three men clearly were? We know through the Christian organisation Open Doors that across the world there are Christians actually having to go through this level of persecution just to worship God and read his Word. Yet we can read it whenever we choose and worship our hearts out at any time. So how do we rely on God? By reading our Bibles daily, praying and learning from teaching. By accepting that God doesn't expect us to be perfect; he accepts us as broken and vulnerable. He loves us. He sent his son Jesus to save us. And one of Jesus' greatest promises in the Bible was in Matthew 11:28-30:

'Then Jesus said, "Come to me, all of you who are weary and carry heavy burdens, and I will give you rest. Take my yoke

upon you. Let me teach you, because I am humble and gentle at heart, and you will find rest for your souls. For my yoke is easy to bear, and the burden I give you is light."

Now if you think of rest, it probably involves a sofa, right? Jesus is also talking about a yoke, which in this case does not mean of the egg variety. No, he is talking about being yoked in a harness. I wrote down this description from somewhere (I have no idea where I got it) of what he meant;

'A yoke is a harness that goes around TWO necks so that two oxen can pull the load. It's a picture of help because you are suddenly not pulling the load alone. In each team one oxen is the leader and the other follows. Jesus will take the lead, but you must be yoked to him for that to happen.'

So, I have two questions for you to mull over right now. Firstly, are you yoked to Jesus? If not, who or what are you yoked to? Is it debt, addiction, illness, success, pursuit of money, your looks? Because if it is any of those they will be about as reliable as the Reliant Robin. Secondly, who is in the driving seat? Is it Jesus, or is it you?

Jesus promises in this verse that his yoke won't choke you, hurt you, be wearisome or confining. The irony actually is if you want to be completely free you must allow yourself to be yoked to Jesus and submit your life to him which is the exact opposite of what people believe following Jesus will be like before they give their life to him. They believe the lies that the media peddles that when you follow Jesus your life will become restrictive and full of rules that you can't possibly live by instead of the truth, that LOVE will pour into you like no other, before or after. So how else do we stay or start to be reliant? By abiding in his Word. Not just reading it but abiding in it. In John 8:31-32 Jesus says to his people:

'You are truly my disciples if you remain faithful to my

teachings. And you will know the truth, and the truth will set you free.'

The word 'abide' here means to remain, to continue, to stay. We need to live in this. I think that sounds so beautiful – to live in his word. And to do this you may have to give up something else. You may have to switch from relying on something else to relying on God. If God is central to your life, then everything you do will flow out of that love. Maybe then you will have the courage to step out and rely on him and him alone. God doesn't want you to read his Word, pray and learn from teaching for the sake of it – so he can see how much he can get you to do. No, he wants that for you because it is through doing those things you will find who you truly are. The awe-inspiring person he created you to be. What your salt and light truly look like in the world.

Through these actions you will see the beauty in each person around you and in yourself. Instead of looking through a filter of worldly, judgemental eyes of what is wrong with you, you will start to believe how God sees you is the truth (and remember – the truth shall set you free). Your relationship with God is an ongoing, lifelong work of art. Giving your life to Jesus is just the beginning. After that, the hard work begins - learning to hear his voice above the noise, becoming reliant on him and being faithful when you can't see ahead and all you FEEL is pain or confusion. That is why he gave us the gift of his Holy Spirit. In John 14:26-27 Jesus says:

'But when the Father sends the Advocate as my representative – that is, the Holy Spirit – he will teach you everything and will remind you of everything I have told you.

I am leaving you with a gift – peace of mind and heart. And the peace I give is a gift the world cannot give. So don't be troubled or afraid.'

What a wonderful gift. So that is the final thing that helps us be reliant on God – prayer. He knew we would need help. Praying each day is such a good way to build on your relationship with God and learn to hear his voice above the noise. Like any relationship good communication is essential for it to grow. If we don't spend time communicating with our partner, it is very easy to drift apart. It's the same with God. I think prayer is just our way to stay connected with someone who loves us. If you don't 'practice' praying, or in fact give him the space to speak, you won't understand when it is God speaking to you. You won't hear his direction and love for you; you won't learn to be reliant on him and him alone. In the UCB Word for Today 3rd October 2018 Bob Gass writes:

'Generally, God won't send a thunderbolt from heaven to get your attention. More often he speaks through your thoughts, a family member, a friend, a teacher, a pastor, a change in your circumstances, the sudden discovery of the perfect scripture, the writing of a gifted author or in the quietness when he fills your heart with peace. So, learn to listen to God's voice.'

So, I ask you now, will you allow God to come in and minister to you and be transformed by his grace? Maybe sit quietly now with your hands out in front of you and just wait on his presence. Ask God to come and speak to you in preparation for the next exercise in this book.

9 come Holy Spirit

So how do we blast lukewarmity away from our heart, our church and the world? Francis Chan said this very challenging yet genius quote in his book *Forgotten God*:

'The entertainment model of church was largely adopted in the1980s and1990s and while it alleviated some of our boredom for a couple of hours a week, it filled our churches with self-focused consumers rather than self-sacrificing servants attuned to the Holy Spirit.'[8]

That packs a punch, doesn't it? The Holy Spirit was always God's plan for us. God is so loving he gave us his Word and the Holy Spirit to help us. He knew none of this was possible in our own strength. Francis Chan's quote is a good description of what happens when we go it alone. God has predicted as much throughout his word as we have already seen in verse 22 of Revelation 3:

'Anyone with ears to hear must listen to the Spirit and understand what he is saying to the churches.'

So, he commands us to be led by the Holy Spirit. The Bible teaches us that when we are being led by the Holy Spirit we can't sin in that moment. We cannot be lukewarm when we are filled and led by the Holy Spirit. Read Galatians 5 for the full explanation but verses 16 and 17 give us a huge clue:

'So, I say, let the Holy Spirit guide your lives. Then you won't be doing what your sinful nature craves. The sinful nature wants to do evil, which is just the opposite of what the Spirit wants. And the Spirit gives us desires that are the opposite of what the sinful nature desires. These two forces are constantly

8 Francis Chan, *Forgotten God*, p55

fighting each other, so you are not free to carry out your good intentions.'

Our human will is gone and the power of the Holy Spirit's love is guiding us when we submit to his will. I find it so comforting, so empowering, to submit to the Holy Spirit's leading. And it isn't a denominational choice or style of theology or worship but a command by God because he knows it is what is BEST for us – best for our souls and best for our salvation. It is how we keep pointed to Jesus. The solution lies in Acts 2 – the early church – it is our blueprint and inspiration.

'On the day of Pentecost all the believers were meeting together in one place. Suddenly, there was a sound from heaven like the roaring of a mighty windstorm, and it filled the house where they were sitting. Then, what looked like flames or tongues of fire appeared and settled on each of them. And everyone present was filled with the Holy Spirit and began speaking in other languages, as the Holy Spirit gave them this ability' *(verses 1-4).*

They were so full of the Holy Spirit that people thought they were drunk. The most amazing thing happened after this. Peter began to preach in the power of the Holy Spirit (which they could all understand as the Holy Spirit had given them the gift of hearing in their own language).

It then says in verses 37-41:

'Peter's words pierced their hearts, and they said to him and to the other apostles, "Brothers, what should we do?"

Peter replied, "Each of you must repent of your sins and turn to God and be baptized in the name of Jesus Christ for the forgiveness of your sins. Then you will receive the gift of the Holy Spirit. This promise is to you, to your children, and to those far away — all who have been called by the Lord our God." Then Peter continued preaching for a long time, strongly urging all his listeners, 'Save yourselves from this crooked generation!'"

Those who believed what Peter said were baptised and added to the church that day —about 3,000 in all.

3000 people came to know Jesus through the Holy Spirit falling on the people INCLUDING the preacher. The Holy Spirit fell, and they received him which then prompted a response by the believers. They were full of gratitude and empowered by the Holy Spirit which is the exact opposite of what we have been discussing and reading about in Revelation 3. There wasn't a lukewarm presence among them – they had different issues, but they were humans like us. The difference was the Holy Spirit. It is impossible to be lukewarm when we are filled and being led by the Holy Spirit.

I want that please. I want to be one of those ordinary people whose life is transformed by the Holy Spirit so I can become extraordinary and do extraordinary things for his kingdom in the power of the Holy Spirit, don't you? Because real, biblical, God filled, Holy Spirit-led love doesn't tell people what 'their itching ears want to hear'. Cancel culture does. Real biblical, God filled, Holy Spirit-led love tells the truth, the whole truth and nothing but the truth. And where is the only place we find truth? - the Bible, God's Word. So next time temptation is put in our way to bend the truth so we don't hurt someone's feelings, agree with an opinion that goes against the Bible or indeed stay quiet; or we justify actions we know do not glorify God or skip church, maybe we can ask ourselves this quick question again: Who do I want to please right now? God or the world? And we can't turn our eyes from the reality of the alternative to following God, to living outside the leading of the Holy Spirit – we mustn't! A brave church faces it head on and I think we can still be a brave church.

Let us briefly look at an example of the alternative found in Luke 16, a parable Jesus tells about a poor man called Lazarus who had nothing. And a rich man who in contrast had everything materially he could wish for. Lazarus lay at the rich man's gate on the floor longing for food, but the rich man ignored him. When the poor man died the Bible describes him as being 'carried by the angels to sit beside Abraham.' When the rich man also died the description is very different: 'he went to the place of the dead.' Verse 23b really drives the message home: 'There in torment he saw Abraham in the far distance with Lazarus at his side.' But verses 26 and 27 really struck me with sadness:

"There is a great chasm separating us. No one can cross over to you from here, and no one can cross over to us from there."

Then the rich man said, "Please, Father Abraham, at least send him to my father's home. For I have five brothers, and I want him to warn them, so they don't end up in this place of torment."

Oh, how awful. How heart wrenchingly, gut twistingly awful. He is crying out for the same thing not to happen to his family. But it's too late. Abraham then reminds him that God sent many prophets to warn them, and they didn't listen, so they are unlikely to listen to the words of a man raised from the dead! Like many of the words in the Bible they speak in many different ways at different times to different people. But I believe the loving words of the Bible are there to teach us and help us along the way, so we don't end up like that rich man and so we strive to help others not to end up like him either. We forget that we are only here on earth for a very short time. But our eternal life is, well ... eternal. We have been sent here to this short life to serve God in our own unique way, keeping our eyes fixed on the REAL prize of heaven. But we quickly get caught up in worldly living and forget this point – worldly comfort deceives us. I remember being at Waterloo station one day. I was full of cold and feeling rough, so I had my noise cancelling headphones on listening to Francis Chan's book on the Holy Spirit called *Forgotten God*. At the time I didn't feel I knew enough about the Holy Spirit, so was feeling prompted to learn more and get closer to the Holy Spirit. A lady was standing in front of me, and I could see her lips moving but my headphones had cancelled out her voice. She was holding a clipboard and clearly taking a survey or something. I reluctantly took off my headphones, sighed and said: 'Yes?'

She asked what seemed to me to be a strange question: 'Are you doing something important?'

I don't know what I expected her to ask me, but it wasn't that. So, I answered her question truthfully (obviously!) and I said to her: 'Do you know what? Yes, I am. I am learning about the Holy Spirit. My husband is a vicar and I work with him. And you know, when you give your life to Jesus it is just the beginning and I feel I need to know and learn more.' (Inside my head I am thinking shut up you idiot, she just wants your email address for a survey, love!) She hilariously then said: 'How wonderful! I think you should be a vicar too.' (I'm sorry but I have to insert a LOL right now because that is not happening any time soon.) However, I then looked at her, really looked at her and heard myself say: 'I don't know what has just happened to you, but I think God wanted you to know how much he loves you today.' Did she punch me? Shout at me? No, she started to cry and then she asked me why she was crying. She then explained that she shouldn't be crying at work. I told her that God's love was unlike any love she would ever experience hence the tears and I asked her to promise me two things. One, that she had heard me say God loves her and two that she would go and investigate what that means. She agreed and that was that.

I am telling you that story so you will hear and reflect on her response. Those were not my words in that moment. I would have had about 5000 more than that. It was a total God prompt. What I forgot to tell you earlier was that I had prayed in the morning for God to put someone in front of me. And he did. Her response was because, some way and somehow, she heard and received God's love for her in that moment. The Holy Spirit moved not just in me but in her too – it was so amazing. I don't know what happened to her next. I don't need to because God has his eye on her. All I need to know is that my role then was to simply respond to the situation the Holy Spirit led me into. Despite my cold and weariness, the Holy Spirit moved because he was a light in my soul, and I had not allowed myself to become lukewarm. 2 Corinthians 5:20 says:

'So, we are Christ's ambassadors; God is making his appeal through us. We speak for Christ when we plead, "Come back to God!"'

So, maybe stand up right now where you are and declare to the Lord out loud and confidently – I am done with the subtle, I am done with joining the world in having an Instagram life and MY church will be a LOVING church. I choose to please God today and every day moving forward. And when you have done that, why don't you ask the Holy Spirit to fall on you and transform you, anoint you afresh and fill you? Do you know the Holy Spirit? Have you accepted that Jesus left his gift on earth for you? Do you want to receive the Holy Spirit now, either again or for the first time? If so, then be bold and put your hands out ready to receive him. Repent (say sorry) of anything you need to and then just wait for him to fill you afresh. I am going to leave the last words of this chapter to the theologian John Stott:

'We do not need to wait for the Holy Spirit to come; he came on the day of Pentecost. He has never left the church.

Without the Holy Spirit, Christian discipleship would be inconceivable, even impossible. There can be no life without the life-giver, no understanding without the Spirit of truth, no fellowship without the unity of the Spirit, no Christlikeness of character apart from his fruit, and no effective witness without his power. As a body without breath is a corpse, so the church without the Spirit is dead.'9

---

9 John Stott. AZQuotes.com, Wind and Fly LTD, 2022. https://www.azquotes. com/quote/827720, accessed June 02, 2022

10 identity theft

Nobody tells you that once you have found faith God starts mixing up your life. Let's pop back to just before we went to Bristol so I can show you what I mean. Just before we left for vicar school in Bristol, I was made redundant (twice). The first time was by phone – that was fun! I actually ran out of the house, I was so distressed. I had no idea where I was going and ended up at a friend's house. I ran because I felt ashamed. I didn't want to see my children and have to tell them I was now worthless. It sounds awful, doesn't it? To think that of yourself because of a job. I wasn't sure why I thought this until a head-hunter said to me something like 'Do you perhaps think it's a problem with you because it happened twice!' Well NOW I do – thanks for that. What a totally unkind and unhelpful thing to say.

But you see what I hadn't realised until that moment was that my whole identity was in my job title, my status and my earnings. I wonder how many people reading this book place their identity in their job title. This experience of being made redundant only sought to feed all the feelings I already had of being lost and insignificant, whilst my lovely husband Ron was training at vicar school, because everything I *thought* I was up until that moment was being stripped away from me. God had taken me to the point where I knew my career was not what I was being called to anymore. But unhelpfully he hadn't let me know what I *was* being called to do. Do you feel like that?

Coming to know Jesus was changing the whole way I looked at the world – and, although beautiful, it was also horribly painful. It was (and still is) like a mirror being held up to my face daily. It is actually progress, but it doesn't always feel like it. It was like I had finally woken up, come alive, and realised I had no firm foundation. My house was built on sand just like it says in Matthew 7:24-27:

'Anyone who listens to my teaching and follows it is wise, like a person who builds a house on solid rock. Though the rain comes in torrents and the floodwaters rise and the winds beat against that house, it won't collapse because it is built on bedrock. But anyone who hears my teaching and doesn't obey it is foolish, like a person who builds a house on sand. When the rains and floods come and the winds beat against that house, it will collapse with a mighty crash.'

I had crashed without knowing why as no one had told me about Jesus' teaching before that fateful night, so how could I obey it? Up to this point in my Christian journey I hadn't really read the Bible properly and completely. I don't know what I had been doing if I am honest. I was on fire for Jesus, yet I was still just faffing about when it came to taking the Bible seriously and reading it. I was still a Bible dipper. Are you a Bible dipper? You know, just dipping in and out, googling lovely Bible verses that make you feel better that day – a consumer looking for entertainment rather than a disciple hungry for Truth. That includes ignoring the challenging stuff like, oh I don't know, ...the whole of the Old Testament. If you are, then admitting it is the first step to not being it anymore. God constantly tried to remind me (in the verses that I did read) where to truly find my identity. Take 1 Peter 2:10, for instance:

'Once you had no identity as a people; now you are God's people. Once you received no mercy; now you have received God's mercy.'

That verse sums up perfectly how I felt. Once I had no identity (well I thought I did but it transpired not so much); now I am God's people.

I wonder how many of you reading this feel like that or have felt like that? Do you feel like you have lost your way, your footing? Or maybe you never had a firm footing in the first place? Then read on: you are in good company. Whilst Ron was coming to life in his calling, I felt the exact opposite – I was shrinking, and I was wondering 'what about me God?' I kept hearing people talk about gifts and calling and wondering what on earth they were talking about. Do I have those? What are they and how do I get them? What is a calling? Does God ring or something? That would be so helpful if he did.

I had a genuine belief I didn't have any. I thought that God's proper work was probably done by all the vicars and chosen people – the super-holy ones. Ordinary people didn't do it, did they? So, Ron did the Christian/vicar thing and said: 'Go on a retreat. That is what people do.' He also said: 'Go by yourself babe; that is also what people do' (said no extrovert ever). Off I went on a hideous retreat. What is it about Christian retreat centres? Plastic sheets? I am a menopausal woman here, not a toddler or incontinent geriatric! Those sheets may as well be an electric blanket to a menopausal woman. The retreat was entitled, 'What are you being called to/what is your vocation' or some such name. So, I went there with high expectations that this was the THING. My first discovery, however, was that people DO NOT go on retreats by themselves. I felt so alone, and I cried a lot. It didn't help that it transpired the whole pastoral team had gone on a training course. How helpful. So, I was on my own (thanks Ron), sobbing on my plastic sheets, which were now awash with tears and sweat. But this was my moment surely – ta-dah – God will reveal all to me. I am Imagining a Morgan Freeman-esque voice saying: 'Rowena, child, you are going to be ...' and that will be like this big reveal by God. This is how it works isn't it? Er ... apparently not.

Paul, the poor man running the retreat, had to spend 'special' time with me as I was such a mess. Yes, you know there is always THAT person on the course. You know the one crying and hogging the (in this case non-existent) pastoral prayer; yep, that was me. They spent the whole retreat banging on about listening for God and I didn't know how to do that and was too scared to say so. I assumed all the other people on the retreat were super holy. Finally, I plucked up the courage to say out loud to a group of ladies who had kind of adopted me: 'Do any of you know what they are on about when they say hear God's voice?' Their response was, 'Oh thank goodness you asked that as we don't know either.' At that precise moment a loud, booming and amplified voice out of nowhere said:

'DO YOU STRUGGLE TO HEAR GOD'S VOICE?'

Well, we all nearly wet ourselves with fright (well, we are a group of menopausal women – sorry guys think prostate ... yep there we go.) We all looked up to the ceiling and were like 'God is that you?' No human person was to be seen anywhere. Then we heard 'IF THAT IS YOU THEN GO TO MEETING ROOM B.' Suffice to say we all went off to meeting room B. Such an instant answer from God to a question, it was hilarious.

When I left that seminar run by the Jesus equivalent of YODA, I started to realise that I needed to learn to listen for God's voice. I needed to learn to rely on God instead of all my worldly defaults that I had, quite naturally, built up living in the world. I needed to look for my identity in God

– instead of my identity being tied up in my job, status, how much I earned etc. As you can imagine I was thrilled to have this pointed out to me. It was up there with the joy of going to the dentist! I am not what I do – I am not my job title. We were put here not to do Rowena's work but the work of Jesus:

'For we are God's masterpiece. He has created us anew in Christ Jesus so we can do the good things he planned for us long ago.' (Ephesians 2:10)

Are you doing that? Do you know what he made you to be? Because it's not just someone who goes to church once a week or once a month! You are so much more. If your identity is in your job title then what happens if you get signed off work – or worse, what happens if you are made redundant, like I was? When it happened to me, I realised I had given him my life, but I didn't actually expect him to do anything with it! I must have naively thought it would just stay the same but with Jesus wedged in somewhere. But I know we were put here with a purpose – a unique purpose that God has just for you. You are so much more than a job title. Think about this – what is the first question you ask someone new when you meet them? It's 'What do you do?' isn't it? If we are honest, it is so we can place them in our minds, learn more about them. Are they clever, rich, practical, exciting…? You get the picture. The church leader version of that is 'how big is your church?' – the question that strikes fear into every church leader. Comparison and building esteem in our achievements are, in my opinion, the main two reasons I think we stumble.

When my children were younger there were mums at the school gate I used to compare myself to. I kind of benchmarked my motherhood score based on what I saw them doing. I used to call them alpha mums. Doing this always left me feeling inadequate. I remember one particular mum I would chat to; she was lovely, but she had extremely bright and overachieving kids (aged three and five) and they would always be eating monkfish, houmous and olives or something with their quinoa (which I thought was pronounced quin – no – ah!). And it obviously had to come from WAITROSE (If you haven't seen Michael McIntyre talk about Waitrose the caps will be lost on you!). She would politely ask me what we were having for dinner, and I would grimace and say 'Fishfingers. Spinach? Yes, mine LOVE spinach' (if I chopped it up so small it was invisible to the human eye and covered in chocolate). And don't even start me on that superfoods weaning book that was popular when my children were small. Her name may or may not have started with an A. I spent endless hours with pans on the stove boiling up healthy mush and freezing it in ice cube trays to try and be the perfect mum and help my kids be healthy.

Do you recognise yourself in this anecdote? Is your worth related to your achievements or what you see others do? Maybe your identity comes from what you have, your possessions? A new car helps you to feel like you have achieved something or become someone. Or maybe your worth is in your status and how much you earn.

These are all identity lies that slowly steal us away from the beauty of who we really are. And they are subtle. They are not always conscious choices – that is why it is good to know which one we struggle with so we can work on it and banish it from our lives, bringing freedom in Christ. I didn't know which mine was until I lost it and fell apart.

I think the most dangerous identity lie of all is the one that means our identity comes from what people think about us.

Are you reading this now like I was and going 'Oh man! I have all of them!' Well, this last one is super common and super dangerous. People always have lots of opinions, don't they? The danger of listening to the many opinions about you is that can very easily go from listening for God in the words people speak to you – to just accepting other people's words about you as the solid truth. There is a BIG difference between these two things and it's a very important difference to understand. We are all called to have people we trust to speak words of 'you need to work on this'; we can't only listen to positive feedback and discount the negative. But being totally reliant on what other people say you are is a slippery slope. I described it terribly the other day (and now I am repeating it) as being like you are on a fun water slide but instead of the end being cooling water, it's poo. Other people's poo they have thrown at you, at that! Like chimps do at a zoo. Listening to who Jesus thinks you are means you come to the end of the slide and are washed clean in his refreshing pool of love, forgiveness and saving grace.

I know it's hard – I really do know that but it is so important we face this identity theft because that is what it is – identity theft. And by facing it and recognising it for what it is – the scheme of the enemy who only comes to steal, kill and destroy – we can then move into the heavenly reality: we are who we are in Jesus, not what we do. You are who *God* says you are, not what someone else says and not what you do or who you *were*. We *have* to let that truth settle in our hearts.

When I was coming to faith, I assumed that all the Christians were sorted/super-holy and it was just me feeling like a fish out of water. However, the more I got involved at church I realised that I wasn't alone – people who looked totally together to me on the outside really didn't know who they were on the inside. All kinds of people – people with nothing, barristers, businesspeople, mums, dads and people married to vicars, people who had been Christians for YEARS. God showed me again that I am not alone in feeling less than, insignificant, not valuable. People all the time were looking for their affirmation in people's opinion of them just like I was. That is a really dangerous power to give people. You see we don't need people in our family, our congregation or community to see what we do/love us/affirm us/build us up when we know Jesus. And do you know what? They are probably not going to do it anyway because they are humans caught up in their own pain and lives. What they might do is helpfully point out where you are going wrong and where (in their eyes) your failings are. And more cruelly, when the enemy is involved, if you are not careful, they will point out very personal and painful things about you that you ALREADY KNOW and don't like about YOURSELF. But I am here to tell you, as painful as it is, it's just their opinion. Just because they said it doesn't make it true. All you need to know is how loved you are by God. Nothing God does is an accident. YOU are not an accident.

I once asked a wise person: how do I know which voice is God's and which is mine or the enemy's? His answer was so good I share it with you now:

'God's voice will convict you. The enemy's voice will condemn you.'

So next time a negative thought comes into your mind when you pray stop and ask yourself, does this voice convict me or condemn me? I would love you to make a choice today as you read this. Ask yourself do you want to be a people-pleaser or a God-pleaser?

We all have lies painted on our walls (as Bob Goff would say) – lies we believe about ourselves, lies spoken over us, lies formed from crushingly painful experiences. I believe these lies affect our confidence, our identity and our ability to hear and carry out our calling to be a whole-life, on-fire disciple for God. It doesn't matter if you have been a Christian for 100 years or you are just starting out, have no doubt you are CALLED to something, but you can't fulfil it until you lay down the lies and listen for what God is saying to you right now in this current season, not what you have always done, what you did last year, but right now. This book right now is your ordained appointment with him today.

In our last church in London, we had a congregation on a Wednesday who were, let's say politely, over the age of sixty-five. I loved them. They were old-school and it didn't matter how crazy their vicar's wife appeared to be, they loved me because that is what you did. They gave me love and wisdom and I was very thankful for them. But I got the sense that some of them felt God had finished with them because they were older and were less mobile etc. That was a lie that they believed. The truth was they had love, wisdom and prayer to give. They could be grandparents to the grandparent-less, parents to the orphans, friends to the widowed. So, my way of affirming this was to shout out to them every time I preached:

'ARE YOU DEAD YET?' (Yes, really, I did!)

They would shout back laughing a very loud 'NO!'

Then I would shout 'THEN GOD STILL HAS SOMETHING HE WANTS YOU TO DO.'

Wonderful and unique you. Don't judge me because, as unorthodox as it was, it worked. I think we need to shout the same question to the global church right now too.

ARE YOU DEAD YET CHURCH?

What would the answer be I wonder? Because if you don't understand who you are in him and what your calling is then this whole life discipleship thing could really take its toll on you and the enemy loves that – it is one of his tools.

'The thief's purpose is to steal and kill and destroy. My purpose is to give them a rich and satisfying life.' (John 10:10)

11 lies down the loo

Lies are things we believe about ourselves that simply aren't true. They can be things that were spoken over us in childhood or adolescence. Or they can stem from trauma or things that happened to us. The most common lie I have seen that people believe about themselves is that they are worthless. The problem with lies is that they hold us back. If we look at everything we do or may do in life through a lens of worthlessness then the outworking of that can be that we give up more quickly, do not take risks or maybe don't even try at all. Why bother? I will only fail because I am worthless. LIE! The enemy uses this tactic to kill, steal and destroy. All he actually has to do is immobilise us for that to happen. to make us inactive. Scare us into hiding. And what better way than to have us believe that we are worthless. So, we are going to banish those lies right now, because we need to make room for the TRUTH that we will receive in the gifting exercise later.

I want you to put on some peaceful worship music and spend some time reflecting on the lies that you believe about yourself. When you are ready, write down three of them (or more if you need to). I think I wrote a CVS receipt load when I first did this! (If you don't live in America, then CVS receipts are about 100ft long and use up a whole tree every time you go in a shop to buy a stick of chewing gum.) I am going to share mine with you so that you know what I mean and feel courage to do the same. These were the genuine lies I believed about myself and flushed down the loo, British slang for toilet, a few years ago. Occasionally I pick them back up but essentially these were mine:

When people get to know me, they won't like me anymore – LIE.

When people get to know me, they will realise I am a horrible, stupid person – LIE.

I am ugly – LIE.

Now to your lies. Be brave. No one else will see them. Just you and God, and he already knows what you are going to write down. Write them on toilet paper in readiness for flushing them away in a minute. This was my lovely mentor's very practical idea as she had visions of lots of people blocking their loos or them not going away. Anyway, when you have written them, I want you to go and flush them down the toilet and ask God to take them from you. I then want you to CHOOSE to trust in that moment that he has. And it is a choice. You can make that choice. I know you can, in his strength. I know it's weird, but it works. It's not a magic trick or anything and I realise that you may well try and pick them back up again later, but it is a significant way of allowing the Holy Spirit to come and take the lies away for you. It is you recognising them for what they are (sewage in your life) and clearing a path to move forward with God into this new season. I believe that the moment your fingers touched this book God lit a new fire in you. Don't let the enemy pour cold water on that fire with his lies. God is getting you ready to receive all he has for you right now and those lies are NOT included.

It says in 2 Corinthians 12:9:

'But he said to me, "My grace is sufficient for you, for my power is made perfect in weakness." Therefore, I will boast all the more gladly about my weaknesses, so that Christ's power may rest on me.' (NIV)

Hurrah and ballyhoo. His power is made perfect in our weakness because in that moment there is more of him and less of us. So, I say bring it on – our weaknesses on display for all to see. Mine are seen clearly every time I come to church and cry, which is a lot, and I would rather be naked than cry in public by the way. A classic example of this was the first day of Ron's new job as vicar at St Saviours in Sunbury. We had moved back from Devon only five days earlier having left our lovely church in Cullompton where Ron did his curacy. Picture the scene: new house, boxes (although Ron had worked like a Trojan to unpack so we all felt at home). We were all feeling a little discombobulated to say the least. I love that word – discombobulated. It describes a feeling of being overwhelmed, upside down and lost so well. Anyway, I woke up that Sunday morning feeling like I had been run over by a truck of bereavement. This is my very dramatic description of how I felt. And in that moment, I had to make a decision whether to go in and paint a fake smiley face on or just be myself. I think you know me well enough by now to know exactly which way that went. Oh yes, no face painting over at this circus!

I sobbed my way through the service, alarming more and more people as the service went on (it's a gift I have). I could almost hear them saying: 'Well this new vicar seems nice but what on earth is wrong with his wife?' So, I crawled over to the prayer area and asked 'Mummy Val', as she later became known to me, to pray. Now you need to know I am not an attractive crier. There was snot, tears, deep breathing – the works. Not like in films where they shed a solitary tear and look immaculate. Oh no. I looked like the elephant man who had experienced an anaphylactic reaction to his medication. But anyway, they prayed, and Mummy Val whispered in my ear at the end, 'Thank you. You have just given all of us permission to cry too'. What a kind thing to say. My vulnerability, my Jerry Springer-esque display of sadness gave all the other members of the congregation permission to bring their vulnerability to Jesus too. Because another thing I have observed about church is that often people stay away when they are in pain. People show up when they are OK but in deep moments of vulnerability they stay away. The problem with this is that we inadvertently allow the enemy an opening to isolate us. It is another of his tools in pouring water on our fire. Isolate people so they feel far from God. I learned a big lesson that day. God loves me. He loves you too; not thinner, richer, funnier, cleverer, more organised, more successful, more powerful, more like someone else. He loves you just as you are. But he does love us too much to leave us there. I love some of Smith Wigglesworth's writing (big surprise he is also an outspoken evangelist!). He says often that if we are not moving forward with our faith every day then we are going backwards. There is no standing still in the kingdom of God. That sentence requires another mic drop after it. It is challenging, isn't it? If you are not moving forward in your journey with Jesus every day, then you are actually going backwards.

I am definitely so far from perfect, and the finished article and God chooses to use me because of that. Accepting your own brokenness is a strength not a weakness, one that God can and WILL use for his glory! God chose you and he uses you because of your weaknesses not in spite of them.

12 Queen Esther and your calling

Take Esther from the Bible. Esther is beautiful and becomes queen, but she doesn't come from a queeny background. She too doesn't recognise she has a part to play in the world for God – she doesn't know her calling.

King Xerxes, the king at the time, had the hump with his wife, Queen Vashti, for refusing to obey an order he gave when he summoned her. So, in a huge overreaction following some bad advice from his advisors, he banished her completely (as you do!) and out she went. After he had done this, he missed her. So, following advice from those same advisors, a search for a new queen began to replace the old one – nice!

Esther was at that time a young Jewish woman who lived with her cousin, Mordecai, who had raised her like his own after her own mother and father had died. Esther, being a young, beautiful virgin was one of the women paraded in front of King Xerxes as a potential replacement for Queen Vashti. It is worth noting that all the women brought before the King were prepared over a twelve-month period before they were allowed anywhere near the King himself. In that time the Bible tells us that she was 'admired by everyone who saw her' (Esther 2:15). Esther was loved by King Xerxes more than any of the other young women. So much so he crowned her there and then as his new Queen. Mordecai, who by this time worked within the palace and government, heard about a plot against the King and tells Esther so she can speak to the King. We can see how God has already placed both Mordecai and Esther in the palace and is helping them build favour with the King, in preparation for what is to come. When the plot against the Jews unfolds

Mordecai is filled with grief and implores Esther to help. But she is afraid. Mordecai comes to her in a key moment and says these wise and haunting words in Esther 4:14:

'For if you remain silent at this time, relief and deliverance for the Jews will arise from another place, but you and your father's family will perish. And who knows but that you have come to your royal position for such a time as this?' (NIV)

Think about it for a moment. God is God, He doesn't NEED her to help him, but it is for HER own good that he calls her to do so. It is what she was made for; it is her calling. And it is the same for you. God doesn't NEED your help, but he WANTS it. He wants you to get involved in the community in which he has placed you.

So, what does Esther do next after Mordecai's powerful words? She goes and spends three days with God in prayer. That is impressive. I don't know about you, but I sometimes struggle to keep still for three minutes to pray. Do you know what her words were after that in verse sixteen of Esther? 'If I must die, I must die.' That sentence is mind-blowing. She spends three days with God and then is prepared to die to follow him and all he asks her to do. What changed in those three days? She sat with her loving Father and allowed him time to fill her with his presence, his courage, his purpose and his power. We all need to know that, like Esther, God has a job for us to do – a unique one with our name on it. Have you sat still with God and asked him what YOURS is? If you wait until you 'feel' ready that day may never come. But if you ask God to fill you with the Holy Spirit and empower you with his calling then whatever happens, you will be ready.

It's because of the courage of Esther in this story that I set up a ministry and called it Esther Ministry. My lovely friend Sal from Worshipping Friends (awesome ministry look it up) was praying for me on the phone, and she said: 'I really believe that Esther is relevant to you somehow.' I had no idea what she was talking about as I was a Bible dipper at that time (remember that from before?). But I styled it out on the phone and sidled off to read the story of Esther. Her story blew my mind, empowered me and inspired me onwards, which is why I included it in this book. I am praying it will do the same for you. Maybe pause right now and read it for yourself if you are not familiar with it. See how the Holy Spirit speaks to you as you read.

I then travelled wherever I was asked and taught about the church finding their gifts, being empowered by the Holy Spirit, and waking up and using them. Now let's keep it real. Before the travelling around I had to step out. So, I asked God how to do that and he just said, 'Try one and see how it goes.' So, I did. A chain of events then unfolded that I couldn't have orchestrated myself. First, friends from a wonderful retreat centre in Torquay offered me the use of their space to support my new vision. Then I knew I had to ring Paul – remember him – the teacher on the retreat? He said, 'I have been waiting for you to ring me.' What? This was two years later. I asked him if he would come and teach, and he said yes but only if I would do one session too. Are you quite mad? I can't do that, I thought, but those were his terms. I then asked him his availability and his only free day all year was the same day the retreat centre had offered me. God is so good, isn't he? I then did that putting-a-fleece-out thing of saying, Lord if this is you send 50 women (I thought my ministry was for women, but it turned out to be for everyone). People tried to dissuade me that 50 women wouldn't come and maybe I should lower my expectations. But I didn't and God sent 65 women. I tell you this to encourage you. None of this was my doing – it was all him. All he was waiting for me to do was stop faffing about and step out in faith with the gifts he had given me.

Hundreds and hundreds of years after it was written, Esther's story of obedience and bravery to serve God, coupled with my friend Sal's gift of prophecy and obedience, gave one small, slightly round in the middle, and big-mouthed woman from London courage to step out and serve God in a new way. Will you let her story inspire you to step out too today? That is my prayer for you. That you too will step out and see what he has in store for you.

Because 'God doesn't call the equipped; he equips the called.'[10] That is what he did for Esther, and it is what he continues to do for me. And it is what he will do for you too, if you let him. God has a calling on your life in each season and I pray that you will start to hear from him today and start the process of discovering your value and calling in this season, your gifts in this season and what that looks like in the world. Only then will you truly be awake and operating within your God-given calling. I once heard a speaker at a conference say something like, don't imprison yourself in your comfort zone. That sentence blew my mind (I know, I get it, my mind is blown often). Just think about that again now. Picture yourself in a cage or prison. Now, I wonder if you still feel the same way about your comfort zone, when you have pictured it as a prison. I suspect not; suddenly it's not quite so attractive to stay there is it? Leave your lies down the loo and read on with an open heart to receive more encouragement. By not looking to the world, friends, congregation, your partner or your boss for your self-worth or confidence you can't be so easily knocked down. Outside your comfort zone is where Jesus lives. Sometimes for us

---

10 From *The 5th Wave*, Rick Yancey; Published by Speak, 2017

as humans, 'outside our comfort zone' starts with the huge task of learning to accept that God wants to use *us* for his kingdom. In Isaiah 40:31 it says: 'But those who trust in the Lord will find new strength.' True confidence comes from knowing who you are in God and how dearly loved you are. With this revelation comes freedom and an inner peace. Quite profoundly and counter culturally, obedience to God brings complete freedom. Sounds odd, doesn't it? – obedience bringing freedom. But in God, it does.

Bottom line: God didn't need to create you; he chose to.

13 bible and gifts – true or false

We are now going back to the 1980's.......... oh yes, my era. Do you know I had so much hairspray on my Kevin Keegan (1980s British footballer) hairstyle, which consisted of a perm at the back of your hair and a flick at the front, that my hair went up like a trap door when the wind blew. Picture one of those trapdoors in the ground that people in a hurricane go hide inside. That was my hair. It also meant that it exploded when my friend accidently set fire to it with her lighter at college. That shows my age; yes, we were allowed to smoke in the canteen at college. Can you imagine that now? But that is a story for another book. Smoking kills kids. I am so glad there was no social media around then. I still have a bald patch on my head, and it took ages to regrow my eyelashes and non-existent eyebrows back!

Anyway, moving on. The true or false game was what I used to play when I was younger in the 1980s. So, I have made up my own version for you to play now in your seat. Below you will find some statements. I would like you to write true or false next to each one. Be honest – no one can see your answer (unless you pass this book on, in which case maybe write in pencil) and God already knows your answer. Just write your own true or false:

1. God hasn't given me any gifts.

2. Gifts are only given to super-holy people and important people.

3. Gifts are for other people, because God loves them more.

4. Gifts are not given to everyone.

5. I am too broken and bad for him to love me and give me gifts.
6. Your gifts stay the same throughout your life.
7. Some gifts are more important than others.
8. It doesn't matter if you are not using your gifts.
9. If it is your gift, then it should be easy.
10. You are not supposed to ask God for gifts.

I genuinely believed all these things about myself and thought I was as much use to God as a chocolate teapot. And none of them are the truth as he sees me. So, it is important to recognise these thoughts might be there but then dump them immediately – just like we did with the lies down the loo. They too are lies again to keep you from the biblical truth of who you are. You can symbolically flush them down the loo with the other lies if you like. You could throw all the lies you believed in this list at God in prayer, whilst standing in your bathroom and then symbolically flush the chain at the end of the prayer in an albeit slightly weird, yet nonetheless courageous act of closure. It is again a powerfully symbolic way to lay this down and move on with an open heart to receive what God has for you next. Without carrying the clutter of lies forward with you. Done that? Great. Let's now dwell on what the Bible says about gifts. Firstly, I love the verse in Romans 12:1 where it says:

'I plead with you to give your bodies to God because of all he has done for you. Let them be a living and holy sacrifice – the kind he will find acceptable. This is truly the way to worship him.'

He is PLEADING with us to give our bodies for his service. By using the gifts he has given us, that is what we are doing. We are being obedient to his call on our life. So, this isn't just about doing what we are 'good at'; it is about fulfilling the plan he has on our life. More importantly it is the way to worship him. I have never truly read that and taken it in before. This is truly the way to worship him. When I think of worship, I often think of singing. What do you think of when you think of worship?

So, by following his call – which is what you are doing if you are seeking his will for your life –you are worshiping him. You are saying 'Your will is better than my will and the gift or gifts you have blessed me with are to be used.' Having a gift and not using it is a bit like learning to drive, buying a car and then not using it (as well as a huge waste of money, may I add). Or saving up, getting a mortgage, buying a house then living in a tent in the driveway. Or going to night school for a whole year to learn a foreign language (think Colin Firth in *Love Actually*) then never speaking that language again. Why would you do these things? The same is true with the gifts God gives us.

The passage in Romans goes on to say:

'Just as our bodies have many parts and each part has a special function, so it is with Christ's body. We are many parts of one body, and we all belong to each other.

In his grace, God has given us different gifts for doing certain things well. So, if God has given you the ability to prophesy, speak out with as much faith as God has given you. If your gift is serving others, serve them well. If you are a teacher, teach well. If your gift is to encourage others, be encouraging. If it is giving, give generously. If God has given you leadership ability, take the responsibility seriously. And if you have a gift for showing kindness to others, do it gladly.' (Romans 12:4-8)

Now let's take a look at 1 Corinthians 12 verses 12-22:

'The human body has many parts, but the many parts make up one whole body. So, it is with the body of Christ. Some of us are Jews, some are Gentiles, some are slaves, and some are free. But we have all been baptized into one body by one Spirit, and we all share the same Spirit.

Yes, the body has many different parts, not just one part. If the foot says, "I am not a part of the body because I am not a hand," that does not make it any less a part of the body. And if the ear says, "I am not part of the body because I am not an eye," would that make it any less a part of the body? If the whole body were an eye, how would you hear? Or if your whole body were an ear, how would you smell anything?

But our bodies have many parts, and God has put each part just where he wants it. How strange a body would be if it had only one part! Yes, there are many parts, but only one body. The eye can never say to the hand, "I don't need you." The head can't say to the feet, "I don't need you."

In fact, some parts of the body that seem weakest and least important are actually the most necessary.'

And in verse 27 it says:

'All of you together are Christ's body, and each of you is a part of it.'

I think these verses are quite clear in their meaning; by exercising our gifts we are working as part of the BODY of Christ. And that means us. They dispel many of the lies that we looked at in our true or false quiz a couple of pages back. But how many of us really believe this scripture?

How many of you are reading this now and through lack of confidence or just plain disobedience are already undoing this scripture? Thinking, oh well, he couldn't possibly mean me. Er, HELLO? It is quite clear. Not just that we all have gifts but that each gift and purpose is of the same value; they are just different. If you need further evidence, then I will give it to you. Some people when they think of the body of Christ and the 'important' bits think of the mouth, brain or heart. But I want you to imagine you are a tiny blood cell. There are many different types of blood cells all with different but equally important functions. However, the main function of a red blood cell is to carry oxygen from the lungs and deliver it throughout our bodies. OK – well that sounds quite important then doesn't it? No oxygen = death! Or imagine you are a little toe. Did you know that if your little toe is taken off you have to learn to walk again? It turns out that toe is more important for your balance than you thought. Every gift is important in the body of Christ. There are no top trump cards in the kingdom of God. 'In fact, some parts of the body that seem weakest and least important are actually the most necessary' (verse 22). So once again God knew we could lose our way and prepared a way for us in his Word. You are all important and you ALL have gifts and skills that are equally important, they are just different.

14 Nicky Gumbel v Russ Abbot

God seems to want me to speak in front of people – it's what I do at church and have done all over the place with Esther Ministry. But I am constantly wondering 'really, me Lord?' I will give you an example. Have you heard of the Alpha course? It is a great course to help anyone who wants to go deeper into asking the big questions of life and the Christian faith. It was devised by Holy Trinity Brompton (HTB), a wonderful church in London and is led by Nicky Gumbel, their Leader, and his wife Pippa. If you haven't done it yet I would highly recommend it (www.alpha.org).

Well, when I led one of the Alpha courses for our previous church in London, I didn't understand all of Nicky Gumbel's references to art or opera (I am a bit low brow). Anyhow, they have this wonderful leadership guide which allows people leading Alpha courses to dip in and out of their teaching videos and pop into their transcripts and 'enter your own story here'. When I read that sentence, I was filled with glee. In that particular week, Nicky Gumbel was explaining about the spiritual atmosphere and all I can hear in my head is Russ Abbot (1980s cheesy TV personality – I have just realised all my references are from the 1980s!) singing the song 'Oh what an atmosphere'. I am going to pause here and let you google that song – go on, you will regret it if you don't. Done it? Are you back? It's bad, isn't it? Yet somehow strangely good. It's also now getting loads of unexplained hits on YouTube due to me making you google it. I apologise in advance.

ANYWAY, what I didn't explain is that this particular group doing Alpha were a group of young mums who had never heard of Russ Abbot as they weren't alive then or were just being born (I'm not bitter!) So, of course I did what any good teacher would do and moved on didn't I? Er, no I didn't. Oh no, I decided to play the song down the microphone from my phone. All the while my brain is shouting 'do the dance, do the dance.' So, of course I moved on, didn't I? Er, no of course I didn't. I did the dance didn't I? They are now laughing AT me, at least one mum said she nearly wet herself (well they had just had babies – think pelvic floor; guys go back to your prostate again!) And all along I was thinking one thought, 'I bet Nicky Gumbel didn't do this.'

But, you see, comparison in the kingdom of God is a killer. Comparing yourself to other people around you will just paralyse you from doing anything at all especially if you compare yourself to someone as accomplished as Nicky Gumbel. Just like us, he will have a story too. His 'stuff' didn't just happen overnight; his accomplishments will have been built over his journey with Jesus. And in that journey, there will have been trials and pain. I don't know Nicky Gumbel personally. But through reading my Bible I have learned how God operates in all of us. How he refines us and moulds us so that when he gives us the calling we have, we are actually ready for it. That refining also means he knows we will seek to handle it in his strength and not just our own. We only see a glimpse of that in people's lives when we look from the sidelines which is why comparison is so dangerous to our faith and can derail us very easily. But thankfully God sees and knows their hearts, the whole truth, their potential. And that means he sees yours too. The mums doing this Alpha course said it was the highlight of the course, which is a bit of an epic fail as the highlight of the course is actually Jesus. My point is that every gift is equal; they just look different. All the different gifts are needed in God's big plan because he has a big plan for us as a community around the world.

And that includes YOU.

I spoke with a friend of mine who works for Tearfund (awesome Christian development charity; find them at www.tearfund.org) and who has a more logistical and office-based role. He said that sometimes he struggles to see where his role fits in God's plan and how it is serving him. But the reality is that if he didn't do what he did many people across the world wouldn't be safe or in the right place at the right time with the right aid. This in turn could have disastrous consequences. Through the Bible verses we discussed in the previous chapter God reminded him that he is part of the body at work at Tearfund where everyone has a part to play, whether a mouth or a toe!

15 missing piece of the jigsaw

I once heard on UCB radio the late, great and hilariously named, Bob Gass (I am such a child), who was an awesome Bible teacher, say these words:

'There is a cry from the Jericho Road that nobody but you may even hear.'

What an awesome sentence. These words really struck me when I first heard them as he is saying our calling is unique. Our giftings are unique to us on that day as we may be the only person that hears AND responds.

'There is a cry from the Jericho Road that nobody but you may even hear.'

You matter – someone else's faith may rely on you hearing that cry and responding. Just like the headstand person did earlier. She heard from God and responded. The problem is we can be prone to thinking that the very famous person will do it instead. You know – *that* famous person. Their name is 'someone else'. And yes, you may not be the only person that hears that cry, but you might be the only person who RESPONDS to that cry. If not you, then who? He went on to say something like some dying thief will be saved if you will just keep preaching through your pain. Ah – that takes us back to our vulnerability again. That requires us to be brave and embrace our calling AND our vulnerability so that more people, like me, hear the REAL story of Jesus' love for them and come to faith. What is another thing that keeps us from responding? I think it's lack of confidence or an ability to keep going and keep your eyes above your circumstances. And this demeanour or default will always point to a place of forgetting who you are in him (the enemy loves it when that happens as it can knock us off course). That is not your fault, nor does it require blame. Life pain will do that to you. I once heard someone say these awesome words:

'Doubt often originates from our inclination to portray ourselves as self-confident. Self-confidence is a concept touted by the world; it encourages us to rely on our own skills and abilities.'

Self-confidence is a worldly goal or accolade. Worship at the altar of self the world tells us. And self-confidence is a lot easier to achieve than the much harder state of God-dependence. Proverbs 28:26 says 'Those who trust in themselves are fools' (NIV). Does anyone else hear Mr T from the A team when you read that? No, just me? OK. Let's move on.

We can always find our answers in the Bible. I think it is always important, if not essential, to dwell on the biblical perspective because that is the TRUTH. If you suffer from depression like I used to it is especially important. You see, feelings cannot be trusted. How we FEEL on any given day has the potential to lead us into a dark place. Feelings are powerful, but they aren't always the truth. How many times do you see on social media empty statements like 'you be you' or 'make yourself happy' or my personal worst 'live your best life'. What do these things even mean? But God's Word is the TRUTH and will always lead you to the light – no matter how small that light looks at that time.

In Ephesians 4:7 it says:

'However, he has given each one of us a special gift through the generosity of Christ.'

He wanted us to understand that gifts were given to us because of Christ. If you ever need motivation for discovering and using your gifts, then following Christ will be it.

Ephesians 4:16 says:

'He makes the whole body fit together perfectly. As each part does its own special work, it helps the other parts grow, so that the whole body is healthy and growing and full of love.'

So, you need to know that your gift is just as important to your colleagues, community, church, friends and family. It is like you are part of a big jigsaw and the picture can't be completed without you. Yes, maybe you are reading this book to find out you are the missing jigsaw piece, and you are an important part of God's beautiful picture, whether you are scenery, sky, building or a person. No matter how insignificant you may feel, your part is important. Stop for a minute and imagine a jigsaw in your mind. Doing that? Now imagine just one piece missing. Ask yourself this – what is your eye drawn to in a jigsaw if a piece is missing? It's drawn to the hole, isn't it? No matter how gorgeous the rest of the picture may be your eye is drawn to the place where the missing piece should be. You are looking at it thinking, 'Where is that piece? Why is it missing?' A missing piece changes the whole picture. God feels like that about you not fulfilling the purpose he has for you. Allow and trust God today to help you realise you are part of his body because then you will start the process of fulfilling your calling in his enormous plan that he wants you to be a part of.

Why don't you spend a few minutes now going back to that jigsaw in your mind? Intentionally place the missing piece back into your picture. Thank God in prayer that he has a place for you, a plan for you and a deep love for you. Maybe you could just sit quietly and wait and see what the Holy Spirit says to you. Maybe you will find the jigsaw you have just fixed in your mind will become a special picture about your future. You may find it helpful to have quiet instrumental worship music on in the background. It can help to focus our minds on him and stop it bouncing around all over the place. It also helps me with the noise left in my ears from my raving days and Covid! I just know our loving Father has something wonderful to say to you as you rest awhile in his presence.

16 Joseph and the amazing technicolor dreamcoat

Writing a book causes you to reflect a lot on your life and faith as does reading your Bible. I am currently doing a year-long devotional that entails reading the Bible chronologically. It's an awesome new way for me to read and experience the Bible. This morning I was reading all about the story of Joseph.

Now, we have journeyed together for a while now, so it won't come as a huge surprise for you to hear I was a major AmDram kid. For those that do not know that phrase it is short for amateur dramatics (Me dramatic? Never) – acting, singing and dancing. It was my happy and safe place at school. I don't know what school was like for you, but I didn't really fit in anywhere. I always seemed to be swimming against the tide, going in a different direction to everybody else. But my drama teacher looked past the noise and saw the potential in me. She understood me, encouraged me and accepted me just as I was which was unusual in my life at that point.

Every Friday after school we stayed behind and practised whatever musical or play we were doing. In this club there was no meanness, no bullying; just laughter, singing and joy – the only time of the week I could breathe and be myself. I was so thankful for this club. We also got a McDonalds, so to be honest that really helped motivate a bunch of teenagers to turn up. One of the most significant musicals we did was *Joseph and the Amazing Technicolor Dreamcoat*. I played Potiphar's wife (well one of them) – how apt! Life was definitely imitating art in this case at that point. I was boy obsessed! I looked for all my validation in what boys thought of me – all the wrong boys too. Basically, anyone who gave me any attention. It makes me feel so sad for that young me now as I write this and look back.

Now, the story of Joseph is all about him and his brothers and how God takes what the enemy meant for evil and uses it for his good. But suffice to say, there weren't many women in the story. So being that it was in the 1980s, picture a lot of can't-sing-or-act boys being commandeered into playing a brother just because ... well, they had a willy and may have been 2% willing (or would show up for a McDonalds!). This was not the age for 'just stick a fake beard on a woman and let her play a man'. I digress.

Anyway, back to this morning. As I was reading Joseph and inadvertently singing the songs in my head, suddenly God reminded me how I felt at that age hearing the story of Joseph in the play for the first time. I cried every time I heard the music of Jacob returning and seeing not only that his son was alive but also what God had done through him. Yet I had no idea why I was crying. This morning God also reminded me of how I watched *Jesus Christ Superstar* on the TV and cried for half an hour after, completely inconsolable. I can see my parents hugging me with a kind of bemused look trying to figure out what had upset so deeply their normally loud, full-of-questions child. I kept saying: 'It's so unfair; how could they do that to him?' My Mum and Dad tried to reassure me, saying all they knew at that point. But what I didn't know then was that the film is not a story. All I knew is it hurt. This morning God showed me that aged twelve or thirteen that incident was in fact my first encounter with the powerful truth about Jesus dying on the cross for us. It was, in fact, the first time it broke my heart. But there was no one to tell me why my heart was broken.

God then panned back to *Joseph and the Amazing Technicoloured Dreamcoat*, and I realised this morning, like a thunderbolt, that the teachers never told us it was based on or inspired by a Bible story. So, there was no one I could ask about why it was affecting me so deeply. With no guidance to the TRUTH, I assumed it was the music and that I am a person who is moved by music and that is was an AmDram thing. I wonder how many other people have watched the musical and believed the same lie: that it's just the powerful music.

As that teenager there was no way I could go and check the Bible and read and learn more, because I had never heard of the Bible. Let that fact sink in. I had never heard of the Bible. No one had pointed me there so how would I know? And that is only getting worse in our society today. At every turn we are witnessing the attempt at airbrushing Christianity out of everyday life for fear it MAY offend someone. Well, let me tell you THAT offends me. This morning my heart broke for my thirteen-year-old self and all the thirteen-year-olds that exist around the world right now. My heart broke for that little girl lost and searching like many others are at that age and still are now if we are honest! I was trying to work out who I was and all the while the answer was right under my nose. If only one of God's people had pointed me to it. And you know if we, as ambassadors of Jesus, don't help the thirteen-year-olds of this world today then the world certainly will! Every day teenagers are bombarded with fake news and world views peddled to them as fact. More scarily is the fact that all of this is now delivered to them via their phones, directly into their little hands – a million fake answers to their deep searching questions at the touch of a button. But where is the Christ input? Where are his people? Well, sadly they are falling asleep at the wheel. They are busy laying the foundations of a huge middle ground motorway of compromise in the misguided view that it is the loving response to a hurting world, instead of leading people towards the narrow lane of truth that leads to real love, wholeness and completeness.

So, my thirteen-year-old self cries out to you today. DO SOMETHING. Help all the current thirteen-year-old versions of me and you out there. It doesn't even need to be big or scary for you to start with. Let's imagine what it could have looked like for me all those years ago. ALL they had to do was at the end of the play come out and say something like, 'if this has moved you, turn to Jesus' or 'if this has moved you, come and get prayer' or 'if this moved you and you would like to know more, then find this story and many more in a book called the Bible'. But they didn't. Can you imagine if they had? What would have become of that tender, troubled, searching heart of mine aged thirteen? Could I have found Jesus so much earlier? I didn't fit in anywhere except in this drama group. My little thirteen-year-old heart was deeply searching for why I existed, and it was there right under my nose. But no one told me. Can you imagine if in the West End at the end of curtain call, they said: 'If any of these words have touched your heart there is a book you can read to learn more; it's called the Bible.' Or they had prayer people there at the front at the end and just offered people the opportunity to pray. I would have run to the front, shoes off to find out what this deep longing in my soul was.

We live in a world that is far from Jesus. We can no longer assume that Christian teaching happens at home or even school. My Mum and Dad didn't know Jesus themselves so how could they lead us to him? Praise God, they found him (way before me) after I had left home. But at that time, I had no one to ask. If all the youth groups are now becoming secular where will children find the answers to the longing that God has placed inside them?

Us.

So, I don't know what your job is. Maybe you are a teacher, nurse, football coach, a businessperson ... it doesn't matter. Can you see how one simple question or mention could have changed my life at that time? There are people around you whose lives could be changed if you will be brave and allow yourself to be led by the Holy Spirit every day in every part of your life.

There must have been a Christian teacher at my school. There must have been a Christian working in the West End on *Joseph and the Amazing Technicolor Dreamcoat*. But they stayed silent. Or were too afraid to speak. The NHS (the British national health system if you are from outside the UK) is a great example of what I am talking about. The current climate within the NHS today implies you can't pray for people, or you could lose your job. One reason touted is that you *may* cause offence – the hard reality of the climate we live in. It's one based on fear, and it leaves no room for God to move. It means that everything you do you are being asked to do it from an earthly level, based on your own capabilities. What a huge weight that must be for all the NHS staff. But as citizens of heaven, we have the opportunity to deal with life on a spiritual level. Remove that burden and hand it over to God. Do you not think God is bigger than your boss? Why have we allowed this to happen? The NHS is full of wonderful and caring professionals, many, many of whom happen to be Christians. Can you imagine what would happen if every Christian staff member in the NHS prayed for every patient they treated or came across? Think about it. Think of the chain of people involved in your care.

It's not just doctors and nurses. It's administrative people keeping your records up to date so that they can keep you safe and track your progress, phlebotomists, radiographers, health care assistants, the people keeping patients fed and bringing a cup of tea to your relative as they wait for news, the people who do patient transport, the cleaners keeping the workspaces safe and clean and the person who runs the facility balancing the books to make sure there is budget so that the treatment you need is available when you need it; the list is endless. But imagine if every person in that chain who had Christian faith as small as a mustard seed prayed when they cleaned the room and invited the Holy Spirit in or the administrator who prayed healing over your file as it came across their desk. Imagine still if the doctor who met with you explained your treatment plan and then offered to pray? WOW I don't think it would take long to see a change. And if you don't believe me let's look to the Bible for an example in Exodus 1. That was my reading this morning as I prepared to send in my manuscript to my editor. As only God can do, he reminded me of a very short but powerful story in the Bible. One that speaks volumes into what we are thinking about right now. Picture the scene: a new king had come into power, and he didn't know anything about Joseph and his previous God-led saving of thousands of people from famine. And so he looked with his human eyes at the growing Israelite people, and he viewed them with fear. He was worried they would overpower him and his men in a battle because there were more of them than his army. So, what did he do? Well, apart from enslaving them horrifically, he made a plan. Without seeking God, he came up with his own human plan. That plan is described in Exodus 1:15-16:

'Then Pharaoh, the king of Egypt, gave this order to the Hebrew midwives, Shiphrah and Puah: "When you help the

Hebrew women as they give birth, watch as they deliver. If the baby is a boy, kill him; if it is a girl, let her live.'"

Nice! But what did the midwives do? They quietly said no:

'But because the midwives feared God, they refused to obey the king's orders. They allowed the boys to live, too.

So, the king of Egypt called for the midwives. "Why have you done this?" he demanded. "Why have you allowed the boys to live?"

"The Hebrew women are not like the Egyptian women," the midwives replied. "They are more vigorous and have their babies so quickly that we cannot get there in time."

So, God was good to the midwives, and the Israelites continued to multiply, growing more and more powerful. And because the midwives feared God, he gave them families of their own.' (Exodus 1:17-22)

They refused. They refused to follow the king's order and chose obedience to God instead. Despite a huge threat to their lives, they chose to obey God. And God protected them. Actually, he didn't just protect them he blessed them. Were they stopped from being midwives? No, God protected them, and they carried on, using their medical training for God. I don't think there is a more inspirational example in Scripture of what I am trying to say about the NHS. When we read his Word, we find all the answers and inspiration we need to take the hard path of glorifying him and leading people to him.

Just before we left to go to America, I had an allergic reaction to a medication I had been given and had to go to hospital. As I sat there on my own waiting at 7am in the morning I prayed for God to send someone with faith to help me. It was the first time since my major anaphylaxis when

Bella was born that I had to go to hospital with an allergic reaction. Surprisingly to me all the feelings I felt of fear when it happened seventeen years prior to this moment came flooding back into my body. I also had a fear I would never move past it. I had worked hard for it not to define me but yet here I was crying out in fear again. Suddenly as I prayed, I started to laugh to myself. I suddenly saw how long I had been carrying the fear of the anaphylaxis with me, allowing it more power over me than God himself. I suddenly saw all the ways that God had held me tightly since that moment and it was like a veil had been torn from my eyes. My daughter was seventeen years old, and I was crying at being in a hospital! Seventeen years later! I literally threw my fear at God in prayer in that very moment and allowed him to take it from me. I was finally free. Right in the midst of another allergic response God was there and he lovingly freed me. All glory to God. Just as I finished doing that the doctor appeared. When he came in, he was very kind. He asked about my previous anaphylaxis and so I told him my testimony. I asked him if he had a faith in Jesus and he said yes. Turns out he was the head of the whole department – the big consultant. I told him that God had sent me there to remind him that he placed him there as a child of his FIRST and skilled doctor second. I encouraged him to bring his faith to his patients and staff in everything he did. The lovely man shared the difficulties of the NHS with me, and I asked him if I could pray for him. His eyes filled with tears, and he said he would love that. He took my hands and we prayed together. It was the most humbling moment. We both cried. He thanked me for the reminder and vowed to change the way he operated at work. I then went and had all the same treatment I had the day I ended up in a coma and then drove myself home in freedom.

What would happen to that man if people knew we had prayed together? Would he get fired? Would all of these people I listed earlier get the sack too? Maybe. But one of two things would happen I suspect. One, they can't fire half a hospital or clinic; on a practical level they would lose so much skillset overnight. Or two, everyone who was fired could set up a Christian facility that treats the symptoms with healing prayer AND treatment. And knowing God as I do, I prophesy that the results would be outstanding and would have a far-reaching effect on the world.

I suspect a system filled with love and healings would draw people to ask questions like I did. 'What is this I see in you? Why is that hospital/clinic having a higher success rate than ours?' Having spent my 50th year of life really ill, and in and out of the doctor's surgery and hospitals, I was desperate for one of my doctors or nurses to offer to pray for me. I was scared and in pain. Just like a lot of people are when they go into hospital or to visit their doctor. Maybe this is why I feel so passionately about this. God often uses our experiences for his glory and to provoke change. Be a disciple to them. Pray, intercede, ask for healing and comfort. Imagine what our health system would look like if that happened. It occurred to me this morning that this is the same in every walk of life. We are all given opportunities to introduce people to God in small and big ways EVERY day. We have no idea how just giving someone a Bible, praying for someone or asking if they would like to know Jesus can transform that person's life or plant a seed for later. Like me they cannot guess. They need to be told, shown and most of all they need to SEE it in us and be directed to the source. Joseph was bold. He was persecuted repeatedly but he didn't give up. He kept going. He forgave his brothers and blessed them. He used the gifts that God had given him to glorify God and not himself. He knew that he didn't just have an administration job but a calling from the Lord. Just like the other unlikely people in the Bible, we are to learn from Joseph – from his courage and boldness but also from his unwavering faith. He never turned away from God. He never blamed God. And he used his faith in every area of his life. In fact, when he finally revealed his true identity to his brothers, he said these remarkable words that we simply MUST learn from:

'But God sent me ahead of you to preserve for you a remnant on earth and to save your lives by a great deliverance.

So then, it was not you who sent me here, but God. He made me father to Pharaoh, lord of his entire household and ruler of all Egypt.' Genesis 45:7-8 (NIV)

Joseph told his brothers that it was God's plan to bring him there. Yes, that's right – the man who had been beaten by his own brothers, thrown in a cistern, sold as a slave, pursued by his boss's wife, accused of attempted rape and thrown in jail whilst being completely innocent. But despite all that he said to his brothers, the very people who had started this whole journey of pain in his life, that it was God's plan.

God had a plan for him to partake in just like he does for you and the people in your life. Joseph saw beyond his circumstances and saw God working. And subsequently people saw God in Joseph and it set him apart from the world. That is how he ended up in the most powerful position in the land behind only Pharaoh because Pharaoh saw God in Joseph and wanted that in his life too. A couple of chapters later after his father has died Joseph chooses to reassure his brothers again. They are convinced that Joseph can only be tolerating them because of their father. So, they drop to their knees again and beg for mercy. And Joseph response is:

"Don't be afraid. Am I in the place of God? You intended to harm me, but God intended it for good to accomplish what is now being done, the saving of many lives. So then, don't be afraid. I will provide for you and your children." And he reassured them and spoke kindly to them.' Genesis 50:19-21

Wow. He spoke kindly to them and promised to provide for them moving forward. Why? Because Joseph lived his life as a citizen of heaven understanding that God had created him for a purpose NO MATTER what happened in his circumstances. What a witness. And God has a plan for YOU today. Will you accept this, receive it and act on it today? Who can you be a Joseph to today? Who can you tell your story too? Who can you pray for and point to the source of healing? Leave this chapter changed and be like Joseph. Look for the good God is doing in your life; look for the opportunities he is placing in front of you every single day to be a bringer of Jesus' love, a light in the darkness, to pray, to listen and to love again.

17 the gifting quiz – it's all about you

Our beautiful daughter kept asking us why she was the only person who didn't have a baby brother. I didn't have an answer for her. How can you tell a three-year-old it's because the thought of another pregnancy scares you to death? But if my life was now Jesus', if I believed what I was learning about him then I would trust him with another birth. I kept thinking that if anything happened to me, I wanted her to have someone. A partner in crime so to speak, like I had with my sister when we were little.

So, we prayed and plucked up the courage to try for another baby. This time I got pregnant really easily. I will never forget meeting my midwife Pat for the first time. She spoke just like my Aunty Pat with a delicious Yorkshire accent and made me feel safe. She took one look at my notes and said, 'I cannot believe you are doing this again – I am picking your doctor for you.' And she did. As soon as I met him, I noticed he was wearing that weird Christian fish badge. He greeted me and stretched his hand out for me to shake it. I in turn ignored his hand and blurted out: 'Are you a Christian?' He was quite taken aback but smiled and said: 'Yes I am.' My response was: 'Oh well, then I know I will be fine. Jesus sent you.' And I was. Seven months later our darling boy, Woody, was born bringing more joy and light into our lives. And now aged sixteen and twenty (at time of writing) my gorgeous young adults still love each other just as they did when he was born.

Our world is full of deaf, inattentive or sleepy spirits lulled to sleep in a demonic lullaby. Ron and I were completely deaf. But in our deepest and most debilitating pain God reached in and saved my life. Not just physically – that was the easy bit. No, he spiritually saved my life and took it from a temporary and plastic life to an eternal one to be spent with him. What a gift. And I will be forever thankful that God used my pain for his good. And I will serve him for the rest of my days in thankfulness to him and our friends who took a leap of faith and shared his love with us.

You are valuable to him. That is why I am writing this book. It is time for you to wake up and rise up into the calling God has for you in this season, *today*. If I can write a book – then you too can do anything HE asks you to do. Starting with his quiz!

You now have the opportunity to fill out a giftings questionnaire. The purpose of this questionnaire is to help you find how God has gifted you today. Right now, in this moment for what he has ahead of you. I pray it will unlock possibilities for you as you move forward.

The Gifts Assessment Questionnaire Instructions

It is important to read the following instructions carefully before completing the questionnaire.

The questionnaire contains a number of statements. Read each one carefully and ask yourself, 'Is this statement true for me?'

Using the following scale, mark each question between 0 and 5, to describe your response accurately.

0	1	2	3	4	5
Not true at all	Seldom true	Infrequently true	Sometimes true	Often true	Consistently true

- It is important to respond to the statement as it is written.

If it says, 'I often feel...' and this is definitely true, respond with a 5. By including the word 'often', the characteristic which the statement describes does not have to be your constant permanent experience to score highly.

- You should not need to spend more than ten seconds on each statement.

Try to record your fast reaction to the question as this is usually the most accurate. As you spend longer you tend to get over-analytical.

- It is important to answer as you are, not how you would like to be, or how you think you ought to be.

If you do not answer how you are, it will affect the accuracy of your final score.

When you have finished, fill in your score on the response sheet at the back of the book. Your score will be more accurate if you do not turn to the response sheet or the gift definitions at the back of the book until after you have completed the assessment.

The Gifts Assessment Questionnaire

Questions

1. I feel such compassion for hurting people, that I actively do what I can to alleviate the source of their discomfort.

2. I often get impressions of God's thoughts and feelings about something or someone, and then have a strong desire to share them with the person concerned.

3. I like things to work efficiently and effectively and get frustrated when they are badly organised.

4. I am able to see specific needs a person has for encouragement.

5. I have a strong desire to help people to become whole.

6. I enjoy getting to know people who are not yet Christians.

7. When I see someone in urgent need, I often want to give to them.

8. I am happier following than leading.

9. I enjoy spending extended periods of time in prayer.

10. I am more concerned with making a person feel comfortable and safe, than I am with making an impression.

11. I want to seek out those who have fallen away from Christ and bring them back to the church.

12. I have a strong desire to bring truth where there is ignorance about the things of God.

13. I believe strongly that Christians have been commissioned to heal the sick and often pray for others to be healed.

14. I can challenge and motivate others to achieve common objectives.

15. I help those who are unsupported and thought to be undeserving by others.

16. Sometimes I experience an instant understanding about people which I did not learn by natural means.

17. I am able to identify and use the resources available to complete a task.

18. I will go to great lengths to seek a person to encourage them.

19. I am able to discern problems people have through the things they say or leave unspoken.

20. In a social setting I often feel more drawn to unbelievers than to Christians.

21. I often find my giving is the answer to specific prayer.

22. I enjoy saying yes to requests for practical help.

23. I feel honoured and privileged when asked to intercede for someone.

24. I feel fulfilled when entertaining people and have no thought of being repaid.

25. I feel compelled to lead by example for others to follow.

26. I enjoy studying the Bible and passing on what I have learnt to others.

27. I have seen evidence of physical, mental, emotional or spiritual healing in people I have prayed for.

28. I am willing to take responsibility for the achievement of specific goals by a group of people.

29. I can patiently support those who are going through painful experiences, as they try to stabilise their emotional and spiritual lives.

30. When I share an insight God has given me, people become aware of their attitudes or behaviour and have changed.

31. I have an ability to see a way through organisational problems.

32. I have a greater desire to affirm the good in someone, than to show them their mistakes.

33. I am interested in understanding more about the

complexities of the human personality.

34. I am confident that people will come to Christ through me.

35. When I know that what I want to share with others is needed, I don't worry about how it will be replenished.

36. I enjoy serving others so they can be freed to carry out their ministry more effectively.

37. When I am aware of an area of need, my reaction is often to pray about it.

38. I am comfortable with all kinds of people and feel at ease with them.

39. I am able to understand the burdens that people carry and patiently help them to mature.

40. I am able to make complicated issues clearer to others, without diluting the truth.

41. When I pray for someone to be healed, I am confident God will touch them.

42. I see the need to prioritise my work and delegate efficiently to other people.

43. I am able to empathise with suffering people and involve myself in their healing process.

44. I am willing to speak out for God and truth, even when it produces an unpleasant reaction from others.

45. I have perception so see how an organisation functions, and I can use this to plan ahead so problems don't arise.

46. I feel grieved when people miss God's blessing because they are discouraged.

47. I find it easy to understand the struggles another person

is going through.

48. I have a deep sense of the plight of those who don't know God.

49. I like to give anonymously to help meet an individual's, or a ministry's financial need.

50. I am a 'behind the scenes' sort of person.

51. I feel strongly that prayer is the foundation of all other work in God's kingdom, and my prayer life is based on this belief.

52. In a social setting, I make a point of looking out for people who seem to be strangers and not know anyone.

53. I am willing to invest time in caring for others and in nurturing their spiritual grow.

54. I want to pass on truths from the Bible so clearly, that my listeners will be able to share them with others.

55. There have been times when I have felt physical sensations such as heat, cold or tingling in my hands when praying for people to be healed.

56. I am able to inspire people to carry them on towards a goal.

57. I do what I can behind the scenes to show God's love to those who are suffering.

58. I sometimes find it difficult to sympathise with Christians who are struggling to maintain their commitment to Christ.

59. I enjoy organising things, so they work well.

60. When I meet people, I try to build up their confidence.

61. I am patient and a good listener.

62. I am reasonably good at telling people about Jesus.

63. I would like to earn more so I can give more away.

64. I feel embarrassed if people who I have been helping draw attention to me.

65. I consider it a high priority to set aside regular time to pray for things other than my own needs.

66. I enjoy making people feel welcome and at ease.

67. I am able to support and lovingly correct those who God gives me to look after.

68. I am analytical and good at drawing conclusions from a wide range of information.

69. I look for opportunities to pray with sick people.

70. I initiate new things that require others to help me achieve them.

71. When I see people in need, I feel compassion for them, and I am compelled to respond in some way.

72. When I share my understanding of God's feelings for someone, I often find they are strengthened and comforted.

73. I enjoy paying attention to detail in the things I do.

74. I get pleasure in drawing alongside people to affirm them.

75. I am able to see things that are holding people back in their spiritual lives.

76. I often perceive the specific need or block that stands between an unbeliever and God.

77. I get fulfilment out of sharing my possessions or money with others.

78. I like to do practical jobs for other people.

79. I get excited when I pray, because I know God works in response to prayer.

80. I like bringing people into my home and making them feel at ease.

81. I have a strong desire to see people grow in their faith and I am prepared to work with them to help them do so.

82. I like challenging others to understand truth and obey it.

83. I enjoy praying for others to be healed and get excited when I am praying for them.

84. I find that I can communicate ideas to other people, so they will want to play a part in achieving them.

Once you have finished all the questions transfer your answers into the answer grid at the back of this book (page 139) then add up the columns vertically i.e.

Questions 1, 15, 29, 43, 57 and 71 add up and write the total in box A.

And so on for each box A–N.

Once you have totalled the 'scores' in each box, turn to the back of the book for the answers - ooh exciting. There is a short answer on page 140 and 141 and a slightly longer description with space for you to write notes moving forward (page 142 onwards).

I encourage you to identify the top three gifts for consideration and reflection and just focus on them. It's OK to have others close behind but just focus on the top three highest scores only. That way it may help you hear God sooner for what he has for you.

You may be curious to know what my top three giftings are and what I did when I found out.

Well, when I took this test again a couple of years ago mine had slightly changed. This isn't unusual if we are moving forward and growing with Jesus. My top gift had become prophecy, followed closely by teaching and evangelism, in that order. Surprised? I was when I got prophecy and I didn't really know what to do with that. So, I decided I needed to go and learn more about it and enrolled on a course. Actually, as only God can do, my husband emailed me a course just as I was starting to panic wondering how I could put my own teaching into practice. I didn't want to be the worst student ever in my own class. As soon as I looked at it, I knew it was for me. It was called 'School of Prophets' and it was based at Bethel Church in America (where I was at the time). So, I took it as a sign and signed up immediately.

And this is what I encourage you to do when you look at your results. Ask yourself the questions - how much time have I spent learning about this gift? Do I need some teaching on it? Is there a course or book I could read? How can I use it more? Where can I sign up to serve in this gifting whilst I work out what is next? So, I did this course, and I can honestly say it was the best thing I ever did. We had to go without some things to enable me to do this course (it wasn't expensive but sometimes we have to give up stuff to make room financially or time wise for the new thing God has for us). Sometimes we have to do that to move forward in our journey with Jesus. But, oh, it was so worth it. I found my tribe on this course. I found out who I was and what God really thought of me, and years of chains were broken off me. And out of it a new ministry was born - the Prophetic clinic. Our giftings require obedience - obedience to God and the new challenges he sets us. I would encourage you to look at your giftings as a whole as well as individually. The new ministry he had me start was all about the prophetic, but it utilises my other secondary gifts too in the teaching of the volunteers and in using the prophetic in evangelism for the first time. It literally transformed my life and I pray that it will do the same for you too.

I want to tell you a couple of other stories about people who did the giftings questionnaire too. I hope they will encourage you to boldly step out knowing others have done the same before you with their set of gifts.

Something I have noticed over the years is that administration is one of the most 'got' gifts. I have also noticed that not all people who get that gift are thrilled about it. I think it's because people think it means they are good at filing. But that couldn't be further from the truth; it is a leadership gift. For people like me it is literally a godsend to have people with the gift of administration around me. It is the ability to look at an organisation and see what needs doing and setting processes and systems in place to make it run effectively. EVERY organisation, whether a church or business, school or hospital, needs someone with this gift. If you doubt what I am saying, then go and read Joseph's story. He was, in my opinion, the greatest administrator in the Bible. Because of his gift (coupled with his faith and desire to follow God alone) many people didn't starve in the famine. Well, a dear friend of mine got this gift; I will call her Phyllis. Understanding how important this gift was to God and subsequently how important she was to God transformed her future. She left the job she had worked in for years and stepped out in faith to work for a church. She is part of the body of Christ using their gifts to grow the kingdom of God. What a gift she is to that church. Understanding that she had gifts and that she could use them for him was life-changing. And it's good to note that she wasn't surprised by the gifts – a lot of people aren't. But what she found inspiring was that they were important to God and could be used to grow the kingdom.

My friend Helen tells the story of how doing the Esther Ministry gifting day and exercise gave her an unusual bump into her next calling. She kindly agreed to write it in her own words for the book.

Helen's story

Towards the end of my husband's ordination training in 2013, I started to wonder if God could very possibly be calling me to ordination too. This feeling kept popping up over the next four years, but each time I would convince myself that my calling was to support my husband's ministry and the Christian cancer ministry God had put on my heart to set up, and so each time I would dismiss the nudges and push that jack firmly back in its box.

In March 2017, I organised a women's 'Esther Ministry Gifting Day' by Rowena Cross at our church in Lancashire, for the benefit of the ladies – to bless them and stretch their faith. In the busyness of organising the conference, I almost forgot that God would have an agenda for me too! In one of the first sessions of the day, Rowena talked about how easy it is for us to believe in lies and to live our lives according to those lies. We were invited to ask God to reveal any lies that we were living by. I was blown away when immediately I had a sense of God saying to me that I believed my cancer was going to return sometime soon and that I could only ever look at the immediate future because I did not believe I would have a long-term future. We were asked to write down the lies, so I wrote down the lie that I believed I would have cancer again and die soon. We were invited to put the piece of paper in a bin in front of a huge cross, and Rowena then set fire to the bucket. It was so powerful and moving, and I felt released. In the afternoon, we completed a 'gifting questionnaire' and the two gifts which came top for me were 'healing' and 'leadership.' I don't know why I was surprised to get those, but I was! We were asked to pray about what we were going to do now that God had got rid of the lies and shown us our gifts, and the words I found myself writing were 'explore ordination.' I just stared at the words I had written and knew I had to be obedient and stop ignoring God's call and do something about it - in Rowena's words, 'to stop faffing about and crack on for Jesus.' I was at the back of the church for most of the day as I was on the sound and visuals desk, and I remember just staring at the cross and looking past it - as if God was saying I defeated those lies on the cross, so now look beyond the cross, to the future I am giving you. It was one of the most profound moments of my life.

Within a few weeks of the Esther Day, I had met with my vicar, attended a Life call vocation event, met with the Diocesan Director of Ordinands, was confirmed and formally started my discernment journey with the Church of England. Five years later, I am now halfway through my ordination training and am due to be ordained in the summer of 2023. I look back with some regret that it took me so many years to be obedient to God's call on my life to ordained ministry, but I am so grateful that God used Rowena and the Esther Ministry day to help me to finally surrender my will to his - it really was the key that opened the door to exploring ordination. I needed to be freed from the lies that were holding me back, as well as to see and seize God's hope for the future, and the Esther day and gifting questionnaire certainly enabled this to happen.

Such a powerful story from Helen and I hope a deep encouragement to you. And finally, I want to mention a lady I will call Rose. She was in her 80s and came to one of the Esther Ministry days. After leaving her lies down the loo and doing the gifting exercise she came to me at the end of the day and told me what had happened to her. When she was about seven years old a teacher spoke some unkind words over her. She had carried these words all her life, believing them to be true – until today. Today she left them at the foot of the cross and said joyfully 'now I am ready for my gifts to be used in freedom'. How divine is that? In her 80s and God still has something powerful for her to do with her gifts. I tell that story to encourage you and remind you again that whatever gifts you have got they are important. No matter what age you are, what circumstances you are in and what your background is. FACT.

At the back of the book there is a blank plan entitled Now, Next and Next Year. This plan is just waiting for you to fill it in. It will enable you to actually plan what you are going to DO with this newfound knowledge.

On that sheet firstly write today's date – that will be important as you come to look back and reflect on how far you have come next year.

Secondly write your top three gifts in the three boxes along the top named 'gift name'

In the 'Now' box reflect on how much time you currently spend using your giftings – give it a percentage. You can either colour in a portion of the box or just write a percentage number in the box. Be honest as this is your starting point today. If you only use your gift for two hours on a Sunday, then the percentage will be quite low.

In the 'Next' box write what you could do straight away to do more with your gift/s (write some immediate steps). This could be undertaking a course or training to prepare; signing up to serve in that area at church; volunteering and shadowing someone already doing something similar; or talking to your pastor.

I will let you into a secret. Pastors absolutely LOVE it when people come to them and say: 'I have this gift and I have no idea how to use it for Jesus. Can you help me?' It's like Pastor Gold!

I will also let you into another secret. Pastors generally want to put their head through a wall when people come up and moan about the coffee time changing, the chairs being arranged wrongly etc!

Finally, in the last segment entitled 'Next Year 'imagine/predict/set yourself the target of where you would like to be in six months' time (or one year max).

No barriers. Money isn't a barrier, time isn't a barrier, skill and resources aren't a barrier. Big challenge. This is your dream-big list. How are you going to fulfil the calling God has placed on your life? Because we aren't here for long!

Try to write anything you may need to do to get there. In fact, the more impossible your dream seems the more you need the Holy Spirit to help you with it. Maybe do this task when you have finished reading the book. Ask God to speak to you as you continue to read so you are ready to write when you get to the end.

I have now left space on page 166, in this book, for your story too to add to Helen's, Rose's, Phyllis's and mine. What happened next for you? I can't wait to find out.

18 Paul, your potential and vicars in their pants!

Paul says in Acts 20:24:

'But my life is worth nothing to me unless I use it for finishing the work assigned me by the Lord Jesus—the work of telling others the Good News about the wonderful grace of God.'

His life was worth nothing to him unless he was serving Jesus. How inspiring is that? It's even more inspiring when you consider where he came from and who he used to be. Like us he was an unlikely person for God to use. He went from trying to destroy everything to do with Christianity to being a significant evangelist of the gospel. Like a lot of us he was in the world enjoying it. More than that, in his case, he was part of the religious elite. But he was so far from knowing the Truth. But God knew him. Just like the man in the headstand story – remember him? God knew who he really was and who he was going to become. God knew his potential. And that is how God feels about YOU. He looks at you and sees your beauty, your potential and the story of what lies ahead. And just like Paul, who did *so* much when he finally found and accepted the love of God that he had previously so energetically sought to destroy, God has a plan for you too. It may look different to Paul's, but it is no less significant. One life changed produces ripples that go further than we can ever see or imagine in the kingdom of God. Ron and I are testament to that. I was sent this Bible verse as a prophecy in 2019 from an awesome sister in Christ who I didn't know before that. And it hit me powerfully that I think it is still for the church now:

'For I am about to do something new. See, I have already begun! Do you not see it? I will make a pathway through the wilderness. I will create rivers in the dry wasteland.' (Isaiah 43:19)

When I got that I knew I had read it before, I even had it highlighted in my Bible, but it was like I had never seen it before.

How is he going to do that? How will he do that? Well, we know the answer don't we – through us! We are the rivers that God will use to make a pathway. There is no other way. There is no plan B. We are the body of Christ in the world. Everything wonderful that happened in the Bible included his people. We are his light carriers. How else are people going to see his love, experience his love and choose his love? I love that in my Bible this section of Isaiah is entitled 'The Lord's promise of Victory' Hurrah! The Lord's promise of victory. Not the Lord's promise of giving it a good try but the Lord's promise of victory. And even more telling is the previous verse, verse 18, which says;

'But forget all that, it's nothing compared to what I am about to do.'

In other words, you think what you have read is awesome; it is nothing compared to what I will do. So, what is the something new? I think it is – Holiness and Boldness where Christians rise up and take their faith seriously, being all in instead of half in on their terms. Christians often talk about revival, don't they? And I think we get that confused with doing something new. You know – let's pioneer something new, 'Let's start a church in a swimming pool – no one has ever done that before.' Yes, there is a reason for that – it's because no one wants to see a vicar in his pants! The new thing is actually not doing something new. It is us doing what we are called and commanded to do. It is us going back to Acts 2:37-47 and doing something old. The way God meant it to be – deeply holy, deeply obedient Scripture reading and following the leading of the Holy Spirit.

It is us being whole-life disciples. It's us using the gifts God has given us and realising our life here is *so* short. I believe revival looks like Christians reading their Bibles every day (not when they can fit it into their busy lives), turning up to worship together every week (not allowing Sunday sporting activities to take over) because that way we are filled up to overflowing from Monday to Saturday serving God.

That way when we leak, we leak Jesus onto people and not the world. I believe that he wants us to be part of a counter cultural move – one that in the 1960s was sex, drugs and rock and roll but now the opposite is true. What is more radical than following Jesus? Think about it, what is more anti-establishment than following Jesus? He wants us to ROAR – not meh! As we have discussed, a spirit of lukewarmity permeates our churches in the UK, a spirit dressed up as tolerance but really meaning anything less than agreement and celebration of whatever the thing is means you are a judgemental .... fill in your own word. Unless of course you are talking about Christianity then you need to shhhhh and stop pushing your views on us. We have a world who tells us the Word of God needs to be watered down and needs to move on with the times – LIES. It tells us that Christianity is outdated and irrelevant at best and dangerous and judgemental at worst.

We did a conference in 2019 and the enemy was so scared of what was going to happen that the police randomly put a cordon around our church and a few streets surrounding it the day before, warning people to stay away, due to them getting intelligence about youths planning a fight (it didn't happen). But that is how scared the enemy was of all those hungry and fiery ladies who were coming to spend a day in his presence. We are his warriors, and we need to ROAR his gospel to our friend crying in the playground, to our broken-hearted colleague at work, to the person you walk past every day, to our children.

Revival means becoming Daniels, King Josiahs and Esthers. Not people driven by fear. Fear of lack, fear of being laughed at or fear of being rejected. I once did some evangelism training and at the end I challenged everyone to come to the pub with me and tell people about Jesus. Now this church had lots of exits and I saw quite a few slip out, but none the less a hardy bunch bravely walked up to the pub. Now, I had heels on so I arrived last, and I was greeted by the smiling group saying: 'Go on then we will watch you.' Now, that is not quite what I had meant but I was like, 'OK Lord over to you. This is proper awkward now!' They even chose who I would go and chat to – a group of drunk young men watching football – hurrah!

So, I went over like something from a Miranda sketch and asked if I could talk to them. We chatted and I explained to them why I was there and gave them a leaflet from the church. I told them Jesus loved them. We had much banter back and forth including the classic question one of them asked me which was: 'OK so does Jesus love me enough to make my footy team win?' My answer: 'Yes if it truly meant you would give your life to him and follow and serve him the rest of your days.' 'OK then,' he said. 'If Jesus makes my team win then I will go to this church.' Now what you need to know is there were only 30 seconds of the game left, and it was 0-0. Suddenly his team scored out of nowhere and this man ran round the pub shouting at the top of his voice 'WHO IS THIS JESUS? WHERE IS THIS CHURCH? I'M IN!'

It was hilarious. I turned round and the people from the evangelism evening were smiling and clapping with him in joy. It was hilarious and I have to say one of the most beautifully weird encounters I have had to date. That is what happens when we step out and leave the rest to God:

'For I am about to do something new. See, I have already begun! Do you not see it? I will make a pathway through the wilderness. I will create rivers in the dry wasteland.' (Isaiah 43:19)

I will make a pathway through the wilderness – that is our country and, yes, painfully it is our churches sometimes too. We are the rivers. God's powerful, life-changing, all-consuming love is the river in us. God can open any door if we let him and believe – he can even make Manchester United win in the last minute for the one he came to save that day. And as someone who spent thirty-four years in the darkness of the world not knowing Jesus, not knowing his love, not knowing his love was for me, I can tell you when I finally met some Christians who loved us in our pain, they were water to our dry, tired souls. They were a river in our dry wasteland. None of them were evangelists by the way (in their eyes), but they stepped out of their comfort zones because they were filled with compassion about our pain, and they told us the thing we needed was Jesus. And we responded. God comes for the one and how many ones has he put in your area of influence. I totally know we do not all have the gift of evangelism, but we are all called to be whole-life disciples. Evangelism needs prayer warriors too, people with the gift of hospitality, administrators to make sure there is a system to keep people safe, people with the gift of healing and many more. It needs people with the gift of giving to buy Bibles and other materials that help people.

God uses the most unlikely people and that is us. Me and you! Choose today to be a person of difference where his light really shines from you and where his Word is a lamp unto your feet. That way people will see the lighthouse within you – within your church, your community and see the hospital that salvation is, and they will run towards it barefoot and eager to learn more, like Ron and I did, and lives will be radically transformed in the love and power of Jesus. I want you to leave this book like Braveheart on acid charging out of these pages, sword of the Spirit in hand and shield of faith up, on fire for Jesus, shouting to everyone you meet: WAKE UP CHURCH! I want you to know and trust that your faith no matter how big or small can move mountains, in the complete knowledge and power that God can accomplish so much through you when you turn your life over to him completely.

19 Ruby's story

I want to finish with a true story of a young woman who came into our church in London three years ago. It was a breakthrough moment in my journey, and I pray it will be for you too. Ruby (name changed to protect her identity) tried the door of our church and couldn't get in. It was a ridiculous door that no one could ever open. So much so that I think the previous vicar had made it into glass so you could at least see who was stuck outside trying to get in. I wonder why no one ever just changed the door itself. Anyway, I ran to the door and opened it and invited her in. She lost her nerve and said her bus was coming. I pleaded with her to come in, but she wouldn't, but said she would come back. It was our Wednesday service for the more mature individual (remember – are you dead yet?). Ruby looked so thin and lost like a baby bird my heart was flooded with love and compassion for her (which was definitely a move of God). So, I prayed she would come back, something I have never done before or maybe even since. Next week I was waiting to run to the door like Fatima Whitbread (or someone who runs – I have only a mum run which is why I don't know any runners' names. The most I can run is a bath).

Ruby appeared and literally fell into my hug and told me why she had come. She said her husband had strangled her until he thought she was dead, then carried her upstairs, covered her with a sheet and written a fake suicide note for her. She told me she was unconscious for twelve hours. This was not the first time this had happened, and her children had been moved to safety because she just couldn't get away from him. But this time he went to prison for his crime. She told me that she had been walking past the church for three months trying to pluck up the courage to come in. She told me that she was afraid. Her husband was about to be released from prison and she didn't know anywhere else to go but the church. She felt drawn to church feeling it would be a place of safety. Now I have the privilege of hearing a lot of stories of people's lives and pain but never have I blurted out the line I blurted out to Ruby which was along the lines of: 'Oh my! Your life is awful; why don't you give it to Jesus and see if he can help you?' As soon as the words were out of my mouth it was like an out-of-body experience of me in slow motion trying to catch them and shove them back in. My brain was screaming at me 'WHY DID YOU SAY THAT? NO! NO! NO! SOMETHING MORE PASTORAL.' I literally wanted to reverse time. But Ruby looked at me and said: 'OK, yes please. I would like to do that. Can I do that now?' I was like 'What? Er, yes.' I called to Ron to help me. We sat with her and explained the gospel and prayed with her and she gave her life to Jesus. She invited him into her heart. There were lots of tears (hers and mine, Ron styled it out) and her face was completely lit up. She kept asking me: 'What did you do to me? What did you do to me? My chest feels different.' I explained I didn't do anything and that it was Jesus filling her heart with his love. She kept hugging me and crying. Oh, how we celebrated with her. I then did what any good vicar's wife does. I handed her over to two wonderfully kind ladies in our congregation who fed her buckets of tea and cake. I also gave her a Bible and told her to learn who Jesus was and then she would know who *she* really was. Start in Matthew, I told her.

Ruby popped back a couple of times over the next few weeks. Each time she was welcomed with joy and her face was still lit up. Her husband had been put straight back in prison, so she was safe.

But about two to three months after she had given her life to Jesus, I got a call to say she was dead.

I cried and prayed to God and Ron prayed for me as I was so upset. As we prayed, we felt the Lord say clearer than we had ever heard him: 'She is with me now; she is safe.' Her mum rang me and said her Bible was open and was one of her only possessions and she had written notes all over it. She thanked us for helping Ruby find God. But this was not OK. How can women be left to fight these fights alone? Well, they aren't. We immediately started supporting and working with a wonderful organisation called Restored, who aim to end violence against women across the world. Please support them if you can for the sake of all the Rubys out there still trapped in their battles. The other thing that struck me was how Ruby came to Jesus. I think of myself as bold for Jesus but how many people had I actually asked if they wanted to give their life to Jesus before Ruby. Some, yes, but not enough. It was like a huge fog had been lifted off my eyes. It was time for me to WAKE UP too.

We don't know how long someone has left on this earth, but God does. And he sends us opportunities every single day to lead people to him, to plant seeds and to water them. Do we take them? Do you take them? What God showed me afterwards is that there are a million Rubys out there. All unique with their own stories, who are wandering and lost. But they need someone to ask them the question. They cannot guess. They need to be asked. Even an atheist needs to hear the gospel once to make a choice. Think about it. If you are going to vote you need to know about the Conservative Party and the Labour Party to decide. You need to hear about both democrats and republicans. If you only hear about democrats or Conservatives, then you don't have the full story to make a decision. It is the same with our faith in Jesus. It is our job as Christians to spread the gospel. We are his light bearers, his hands and feet on earth. Romans 10:8-15 says:

'In fact, it says: "The message is very close at hand; it is on your lips and in your heart."

And that message is the very message about faith that we preach: If you openly declare that Jesus is Lord and believe in your heart that God raised him from the dead, you will be saved. For it is by believing in your heart that you are made right with God, and it is by openly declaring your faith that you are saved. As the Scriptures tell us, 'Anyone who trusts in him will never be disgraced. Jew and Gentile are the same in this respect. They have the same Lord, who gives generously to all who call on him. For 'Everyone who calls on the name of the Lord will be saved.

But how can they call on him to save them unless they believe in him? And how can they believe in him if they have never heard about him? And how can they hear about him unless someone tells them? And how will anyone go and tell them without being sent? That is why the Scriptures say: "How beautiful are the feet of messengers who bring good news!"'

How beautiful are the feet of the messengers who bring the good news. All God is asking you to do is share what you know. Share your story like I have in this book. Their response is not your responsibility; that is between them and God. Ron and I realised that we didn't do that enough. So, we changed that day. We made a commitment to ask every person we met, ask at every service, at the foodbank (we in fact started a service in the middle of our foodbank – it was my favourite time of the week) and we went out on the streets and asked people and so much more. We were not all evangelists. Our message was not perfect. But we saw hundreds of people give their life to Jesus and all the glory goes to God. We were not specially anointed or slick; we just intentionally asked, do you want to give your life to Jesus? And when we were afraid or under attack we thought of Ruby. Of how Jesus worked in her heart long before we met her. He told her church was a place of safety, the lighthouse I mentioned earlier. He opened her heart ready to receive the good news. All we had to do was ask. Will you leave this book and ask? Will you speak to the Rubys God puts into your life? Their stories may be different to hers but they are the ones who need the unique gift and call God has placed upon *your* life. Will you speak to the Rubys who need to hear YOUR story? I urge you to make this your goal as you move forward. I celebrate all you will do, and I cannot wait to hear your story following this book. As you step forward to be bold, stop faffing and crack on for Jesus!

A first step you can take right now is to pray this prayer of recommitment to God. Say the words out loud, open your heart and let the Holy Spirit minister to you. Ask him for a new vision for this new season. Sit and wait for him to speak to you.

You could put your hands out in front of you ready to receive from him. It is your way of saying I believe you love me; you have given me gifts and you want me to use them so I give my life back to you again right now for your service moving forward in love.

Dear God,

I want to recommit my life to you today. Please help me to become the person you created me to be. Enable me to always live a life that is pleasing to you.

I want to be a witness to others of your saving grace and power. Forgive me when I take back the control of my life. I want you to be Lord of my life.

Renew my passion to walk more closely with you. You know all my desires and plans. Help me to fulfil your unique call and purpose in my life.

Renew my heart, restore the joy of my salvation and grant me a willing spirit to sustain me. Lord, thank you for the hope I have in you. Use my life to bring you glory, honour and praise.

Thank you, Lord Jesus for hearing and answering my prayer. In Your Name.

Amen. Amen. Amen.

The gifts assessment questionnaire

Results

When you have responded to each statement on the assessment form, transfer your score onto the table below, writing your score for each statement into the numbered box. Total each column in the highlighted box at the bottom of the column.

Each column relates to a specific gift. Note the three highest scores and refer to the gift definitions to see which they refer to.

1	2	3	4	5	6	7	8	9	10	11	12	13	14
15	16	17	18	19	20	21	22	23	24	25	26	27	28
29	30	31	32	33	34	35	36	37	38	39	40	41	42
43	44	45	46	47	48	49	50	51	52	53	54	55	56
57	58	59	60	61	62	63	64	65	66	67	68	69	70
71	72	73	74	75	76	77	78	79	80	81	82	83	84
A	B	C	D	E	F	G	H	I	J	K	L	M	N

Checking against the list on the next page, the three top scoring gifts are:

First:..

Second:......................................

Third:.......................................

Spiritual Gifts Assessment Definitions

A. Mercy
The special ability the Holy Spirit gives to respond compassionately to the needs of others.

B. Prophecy
The special ability the Holy Spirit gives to receive and communicate God's specific message to an individual, or a group, in a way which touches the hearts of the hearers and brings conviction and change, or strengthening, encouragement or comfort.

C. Administration
The special ability the Holy Spirit gives to perceive the way an organisation works and to conceive and implement procedures that maximise the church's ability to function effectively.

D. Encouragement
The special ability the Holy Spirit gives to draw alongside another person to affirm, support and strengthen them.

E. Counselling
The special ability the Holy Spirit gives to perceive and understand blocks to personal wholeness and to enable

individuals to move on in their journey towards personal maturity.

F. Evangelism
The special ability the Holy Spirit gives to impart skilfully the good news of Christ to unbelievers in such a way that they are able to respond in faith.

G. Giving
The special ability the Holy Spirit gives to share generously what you have with others.

H. Helps
The special ability the Holy Spirit gives to find spiritual meaning and fulfilment in undertaking practical jobs that enable the body of Christ to function effectively.

I. Intercession
The special ability the Holy Spirit gives to pray consistently and with faith on behalf of others often for extended periods of time and with higher-than-average confidence that God will move in prayer.

J. Hospitality
The special ability the Holy Spirit gives to make people feel welcome, accepted and safe in a variety of settings.

K. Pastoring
The special ability the Holy Spirit gives to nurture those whom God has given to your care, so they are built up in their faith in a loving manner.

L. Teaching
The special ability the Holy Spirit gives to impart God's truth, as found in Scripture, in a practical, clear and relevant manner.

M. Healing
The special ability the Holy Spirit gives to be a channel through which God bridges supernatural healing.

N. Leadership
The special ability the Holy Spirit gives to recognise and communicate God's purposes and to accomplish them through the motivation and direction of a group of people.

Spiritual Gift of Mercy

Short Definition
The special ability the Holy Spirit gives to respond compassionately to the needs of others.

Extended Definition
All Christians are called to be merciful because God has been merciful to us (Matthew 18:33; Ephesians 2:4-6). The Greek word for the spiritual gift of mercy is Eleeo. It means to be patient and compassionate toward those who are suffering or afflicted. The concern for the physical as well as spiritual need of those who are hurting is covered by the gift of mercy.

Those with this gift have great empathy for others in their trials and sufferings. They are able to come alongside people over extended periods of time and see them through their healing process. They are truly and literally the hands and feet of God to the afflicted.

The Holy Spirit gives the spiritual gift of mercy to some in the church to love and assist those who are suffering and to walk with them until the Lord allows their burden to be lifted. The gift of mercy is founded in God's mercy towards us as sinners and is consistently expressed with measurable compassion.

Those with this gift can 'weep with those who weep' (Romans 12:15) and 'bear one another's burdens' (Galatians 6:2). They are sensitive to the feelings and circumstances of others and can quickly discern when someone is not doing well.

They are typically good listeners and feel the need to simply 'be there' for others. See Romans 12:8, Matthew 5:7; Luke 10:30-37; James 3:17; Jude 22-23.

Thoughts – how do I use this gift? How can I use it more? How could I develop it and use it more effectively? What support do I need to ask for?

Spiritual Gift of Prophecy

Short Definition
The special ability the Holy Spirit gives to receive and communicate God's specific message to an individual, or a group, in a way which touches the hearts of the hearers and brings conviction and change or strengthening, encouragement or comfort.

Extended Definition
The spiritual gift of prophecy is an extraordinary and unique gift. Paul says in 1 Corinthians 14:1 to 'Pursue love, and earnestly desire the spiritual gifts, especially that you may

prophesy.' This gift is a blessing to the church and should not be quenched or despised (1 Thessalonians 5:20). Those who have the gift of prophecy differ from the office of a prophet. Prophecy is a gift from God whereas the office of a prophet is a calling. The Bible teaches us that God wants his whole church to operate in the prophetic. Check out 1 Corinthians 14 for his word on that.

The Greek word for the gift of prophecy is propheteia which is the ability to receive a divinely inspired message and deliver it to others in the church. These messages can take the form of exhortation, correction, disclosure of secret sins, prediction of future events, comfort, inspiration, or other revelations given to equip and edify the body of Christ. All words given need to be taken to the Lord and weighed by the receiver. However sometimes the Holy Spirit will pierce one's heart immediately and let you know the word was from the Lord.

The Holy Spirit gives the gift of prophecy to some believers to make God's heart known and to edify the church. This gift is for the benefit of both believers and unbelievers and is a sign that God is truly among his church (1 Corinthians 14:22-25). Those with this gift are sensitive to both the prompting of the Holy Spirit and the needs of the church body. They should be humble and continually study the Scriptures in order to test these revelations before speaking them. When they do speak, they should allow and even expect others to weigh what is said against the Scriptures and interpret the message accordingly. In this way the church may be continually built up together in unity (1 Corinthians 14:4, 26). See also Romans 12:6, 1 Corinthians 12:10, 14:1-5, Ephesians 4:11-12, 1 Peter 4:10-11.

Thoughts – how do I use this gift? How can I use it more? How could I develop it and use it more effectively? What support do I need to ask for?

Spiritual Gift of Administration

Short Definition
The special ability the Holy Spirit gives to perceive the way an organisation works and to conceive and implement procedures that maximise the church's ability to function effectively.

Extended Definition
The Greek word for the spiritual gift of administration is Kubernesis. This is a unique term that refers to a shipmaster or captain. The literal meaning is 'to steer', or 'to rule or govern'. It carries the idea of someone who guides and directs a group of people toward a goal or destination. We see variations of this word in verses like Acts 27:11, and Revelation 18:17.

With this gift the Holy Spirit enables certain Christians to organise, direct, and implement plans to lead others in the various ministries of the church. This gift is closely related to the gift of leadership but is more goal or task oriented and is also more concerned with details and organisation. See also the story of Joseph in Genesis; I Corinthians 12:28, Titus 1:4-5.

Thoughts – how do I use this gift? How can I use it more? How could I develop it and use it more effectively? What support do I need to ask for?

Spiritual Gift of Encouragement

Short Definition
The special ability the Holy Spirit gives to draw alongside another person to affirm, support and strengthen them.

Extended Definition
The Greek word for this gift is Parakaleo. It means to beseech, exhort, call upon, to encourage and to strengthen. The primary means of exhortation is to remind the hearer of the powerful and amazing work of God in Christ, particularly in regard to the saving work of Jesus in the atonement. We see Paul commanding Titus to use this gift in Titus 1:9 and throughout chapter 2, particularly Titus 2:11-15. He also charges Timothy in 2 Timothy 4:2.

The Spirit of God gives this gift to people in the church to strengthen and encourage those who are wavering in their faith. Those with the gift of exhortation can uplift and motivate others as well as challenge and rebuke them in order to foster spiritual growth and action. The goal of the encourager is to see everyone in the church continually building up the body of Christ and glorifying God. See also Romans 12:8, Acts 11:23-24; 14:21-22; 15:32.

Thoughts – how do I use this gift? How can I use it more? How could I develop it and use it more effectively? What support do I need to ask for?

Spiritual Gift of Counselling

Short Definition
The special ability the Holy Spirit gives to perceive and understand blocks to personal wholeness and to enable individuals to move on in their journey towards personal maturity.

Extended Definition
The spiritual gift of counselling doesn't have a long definition. It is an anointed gift and next steps could include investigating Christian courses in counselling to use this gift further for his kingdom. There is also a huge need for pastoral care in most churches and this gift would be particularly welcome in this area.

Counsellors are like those with the pastoring gift because their calling and gifting are much like those who shepherd and care for sheep. They are called and gifted to care for the spiritual well-being of a local body of God's people.

Thoughts – how do I use this gift? How can I use it more? How could I develop it and use it more effectively? What support do I need to ask for?

Spiritual Gift of Evangelism

Short Definition
The special ability the Holy Spirit gives to impart skilfully the good news of Christ to unbelievers in such a way that they can respond in faith

Extended Definition
All Christians are called to evangelise and reach out to the lost with the gospel (Matthew 28:18-20), but some are given an extra measure of faith and effectiveness in this area.

The spiritual gift of evangelism is found in Ephesians 4:11-12 where Paul says that Jesus 'gave the apostles, the prophets, the evangelists, the shepherds and teachers, to equip the saints for the work of ministry, for building up the body of Christ.' The Greek word for evangelists is Euaggelistes which means 'one who brings good news'. This word is only found in two other places in the New Testament: Acts 21:8 and 2 Timothy 4:5.

Evangelists are given the unique ability by the Holy Spirit to clearly and effectively communicate the gospel of Jesus Christ to others. They are burdened in their hearts for the lost and will go out of their way to share the truth with them.

Evangelists can overcome the normal fear of rejection and engage non-believers in meaningful conversations about Jesus. Their gift allows them to communicate with all types of people and therefore they receive a greater response to the message of salvation through Jesus Christ. They continually seek out relationships with those who don't know Jesus and are open to the leading of the Holy Spirit to approach different people. They love giving free treasure away for Jesus (2 Corinthians 4:7), and it brings them great joy knowing that the 'feet that bring good news 'are beautiful to those who believe (Isaiah 52:7). See Ephesians 4:11, Acts 8:5-12, 26-40, 21:8, Matthew 28:18-20.

Thoughts – how do I use this gift? How can I use it more? How could I develop it and use it more effectively? What support do I need to ask for?

Spiritual Gift of Giving

Short Definition
The special ability the Holy Spirit gives to share generously what you have with others

Extended Definition
The Greek word for the spiritual gift of giving is Metadidomi. It simply means 'to impart' or 'to give'. However, this word is accompanied in Romans 12:8 by another descriptive word: Haplotes. This word tells us much more about the kind of giving that is associated with this gift. The word Haplotes means 'sincerely, generously and without pretence or hypocrisy'.

The Holy Spirit imparts this gift to some in the church to meet the various needs of the church and its ministries, missionaries, or people who do not have the means to provide fully for themselves.

The goal is to encourage and provide, giving all credit to God's love and provision. Those with this gift love to share with others the overflow of blessings God has given them. They are typically very hospitable and will seek out ways and opportunities to help others. They are also excellent stewards and will often adjust their lifestyles in order to give more to the spread of the gospel and the care of the needy. They are grateful when someone shares a need with them and are always joyful when they can meet that need. See Romans 12:8, 13, 2 Corinthians 8:1-5; 9:6-15; Acts 4:32-37, Galatians 4:15, Philippians 4:10-18.

Thoughts – how do I use this gift? How can I use it more? How could I develop it and use it more effectively? What support do I need to ask for?

Spiritual Gift of Helps

Short Definition
The special ability the Holy Spirit gives to find spiritual meaning and fulfilment in undertaking practical jobs that enable the body of Christ to function effectively.

Extended Definition
The spiritual gift of helps or service, covers a wide range of activities in its application. There are two Greek words for this gift. The first one, found in Romans 12:7, is Diakonia. The basic meaning of this word is 'to wait at tables', 'but it is most often translated in the Bible as 'ministry'. It refers to any act of service done in genuine love for the edification of the community. The word Antilepsis is translated 'helping' and is found in 1 Corinthians 12:28. It has a similar meaning: to help or aid in love within the community.

The Holy Spirit endows some believers with this gift to fill the many gaps of ministry and meet the needs of the church as it fulfils the Great Commission. The goal is to energise the church and free up others to use their gifts to the fullest. The result is the continued edification of the church and the added ability to see beyond its own needs and reach out into the community.

We see people with this gift in passages like Acts 6:1-7, 1 Corinthians 16:15-16, and many others. Those with the gift of service are committed to the spread of the gospel. They serve in ways that benefit others with different gifts and ministries that are more public. They have a heart devoted to Jesus and a desire to follow his command and example in Matthew 20:25-28 (cf. Mark 10:42-45). Those with this gift do not seek recognition or a position in the 'spotlight'; they just love to help out. They are content with serving in the background knowing that their contribution will bless the church, display the love of Christ to the world, and bring glory to God. See also Romans 12:7, 1 Corinthians 12:4-7; 28, Acts 20:35; 2 Timothy 4:11; Revelation 2:19.

Thoughts – how do I use this gift? How can I use it more? How could I develop it and use it more effectively? What support do I need to ask for?

Spiritual Gift of Intercession

Short Definition
The special ability the Holy Spirit gives to pray consistently and with faith on behalf of others often for extended periods of time and with higher-than-average confidence that God will move in prayer.

Extended Definition
The burden and ability to consistently pray and plead on behalf of and for others.

People with this gift spend more time in prayer on a regular basis (possibly 4-8 hours a day) than other who do not have the gift. They describe it as work; it is physically and mentally demanding, but it is also the most enjoyable thing in the world.

Intercession involves a combination of identification, agony, wrestling and authority that those without the gift can seldom if ever experience or even identify with.

Intercessors engage in petition on behalf of people who do not know God or for situations that relate to the needs of the world.

They are Christians who know how to walk in the presence of God and to hold ono him for his intervention into whatever circumstances is the focus of their prayers.

When intercessors pray things happen. They know what it is to be prompted to pray and they act in obedience.

Intercessors cannot have a higher calling; they follow in the steps of Christ who continues to intercede for his people. They are fulfilling Christ's exhortation to pray for the many workers required to be active in mission and service.

More on the gift can be found in James 5:14-16, 1 Timothy 2:1-2, Colossians 1:9-12, Colossians 4:12-13, Acts 12:12, Luke 22:41-44

Thoughts – how do I use this gift? How can I use it more? How could I develop it and use it more effectively? What support do I need to ask for?

Spiritual Gift of Hospitality

Short Definition
The special ability the Holy Spirit gives to make people feel welcome, accepted and safe in a variety of settings

Extended Definition
The heart, ability and personality to provide and care for others, using appropriate facilities to offer fellowship, food and shelter.

Such people create an environment where people 'feel at home' and welcome. Their genuine interest and practical care provide a sense of security and strength, a place where people can relax in mind, spirit and body, creating an atmosphere of trust and healing.

People with the gift of hospitality use what facilities they have, and the personality and gifting given to them to bring refreshment. It is often an environment where God's people can be ministered to and encouraged.

See Acts 16:14-15, Romans 12: 9-13, 16,23, Hebrews 13:1-2, 1 Peter 4:9.

Thoughts – how do I use this gift? How can I use it more? How could I develop it and use it more effectively? What support do I need to ask for?

Spiritual Gift of Pastoring

Short Definition
The special ability the Holy Spirit gives to nurture those whom God has given to your care, so they are built up in their faith in a loving manner.

Extended Definition
The spiritual gift of pastor or pastor/shepherd is one that carries many different responsibilities. This gift is closely related to the spiritual gifts of leadership and teaching. The Greek word for pastor is Poimen and simply means shepherd or overseer.

In the biblical context, shepherds had several different responsibilities to their sheep and, ultimately, to the owner of the sheep. They kept a look out for predators and protected the sheep from attackers. They cared for wounded and sick sheep, nursing them back to health. They rescued them if they became lost or trapped. They spent enormous amounts of time with them guiding them to places of nourishment and rest. The result was a trust and relationship that kept the sheep following the shepherd. The sheep were attuned to the shepherd's voice to the point that even if they were temporarily mixed with another herd, at the call of the shepherd they would separate and follow him.

Pastors are called shepherds because their calling and gifting are much like those who care for sheep. They are called and gifted to care for the spiritual well-being of a local body of God's people. Pastors are first and foremost servants. They are servants of God and servants of his bride, the church. They are given a mixture of abilities by grace that allows them to serve the needs of an entire community.

The goal of the pastor is to reveal the glory of God in Christ by the power of the Holy Spirit to a people who need God's grace for life. The primary way the pastor will do this is by teaching the Word of God to the church. The gift of pastor is directly linked to the gift of teaching in Ephesians 4:11 and elsewhere. In fact, this gift could be called the gift of pastor-teacher. The ability to teach the Scriptures is also one of the many requirements of being an overseer (1 Timothy 3:1-7; Titus 1:6-9). By teaching the Scriptures to the church, the pastor feeds the 'sheep 'of God.

The Holy Spirit gives the spiritual gift of pastor to some in the church to humbly teach them, guide them, protect them, and to lead them in the mission that God has for his church, namely the Great Commission. The pastor loves the gospel of Jesus Christ and puts it at the centre of his life and ministry. Pastors do not seek fame or recognition for themselves, but they are placed in a position of authority by the Holy Spirit. The role of a pastor is one of humility and service as he is reminded daily of his overwhelming need of God's grace for the task at hand. See also Ephesians 4:11; Jeremiah 3:15; Acts 20:28; John 10:11-18.

Thoughts – how do I use this gift? How can I use it more? How could I develop it and use it more effectively? What support do I need to ask for?

Spiritual Gift of Teaching

Short Definition

The special ability the Holy Spirit gives to impart God's truth, as found in Scripture, in a practical, clear and relevant manner

Extended Definition

The spiritual gift of teaching is one that carries a heavy responsibility in the church. In fact, James 3:1 warns, 'Not many of you should become teachers, my brothers, for you know that we who teach will be judged with greater strictness.' Like every believer, teachers are to be stewards of every word that comes out of their mouths. But the greater responsibility to which they are called is to be stewards of the Word of God to his people. Teachers have been entrusted with the task of effectively communicating what the Bible says, what it means, and how we as followers of Jesus Christ are to apply it to our lives here and now.

The Greek word for those with the spiritual gift of teaching is didaskalos. From the root of this word, we get our English word, 'didactic'. The word didasko means to teach, instruct, instil doctrine, explain and expound. Those with the spiritual gift of teaching love to study the word of God for extended periods of time. They consume the Scriptures as food for their hearts, souls and minds with the express purpose of knowing him and then making him known to others. They want to know what God has revealed of himself and what he requires of us as people created in his image. They take great joy and satisfaction in seeing others learn and apply the truth of God's word to their lives. They love to see how the gospel is woven throughout the Scriptures and how it glorifies and magnifies Jesus Christ in the hearts and lives of those who love him by grace.

The Holy Spirit gives certain people the spiritual gift of teaching so that they would help the church fulfil her ministry as 'a pillar and buttress of the truth' (1 Timothy 3:15). Without this gift, the church would quickly fall into error and sin. Teachers are there to make sure that doesn't happen. They hate when Scripture is abused and used out of context or with ill intent. They love the truth and speak the truth in love. They will never hide or withhold it. On the contrary, they desire to follow in the footsteps of Jesus who taught in the synagogues and in the Temple as well as anywhere the people were gathered. They are called to demonstrate God's love while revealing his truth to the world without fear. The effect of their ministry is the upholding of God's Word and the growth and maturity of his Bride until the day of his return. See also Ephesians 4:11; 1 Corinthians 12:28; Romans 12:7; James 3:1.

Thoughts – how do I use this gift? How can I use it more? How could I develop it and use it more effectively? What support do I need to ask for?

Spiritual Gift of Healing

Short Definition
The special ability the Holy Spirit gives to be a channel through which God bridges supernatural healing

Extended Definition

The spiritual gift of healing found in 1 Corinthians 12:9 is actually plural in the Greek. Charismata iamaton is literally translated 'gifts of healings'. All spiritual gifts are to be exercised in faith, but gifts of healings involve a special measure of it. This gift is interesting in that there is no guarantee that a person will always be able to heal anyone he or she desires. It is subject to the sovereign will of God, as all spiritual gifts are.

The disciples were given authority to heal and cast out demons, but they were not always successful. The Apostle Paul was not able to heal himself and was told that God's grace was enough to carry him through his infirmity without removing it from him (2 Corinthians 12:7-10). This gift is given at various times and places to reveal the God of heaven to the sick and tormented. If healing is not granted, then we can conclude that God has greater plans for letting the person go through the illness or infirmity.

The spiritual gift of healing is an intimate one as it reveals the heart and compassion of God. Jesus is the Great Healer and Physician and during his ministry on earth he healed countless people and cast out demons (Matthew 4:23-24; 8:16; 9:35, Mark 1:34). Healings reveal that God is near to his people and he cares about their sufferings. Healings are meant to draw people to God through his Son Jesus Christ. God wants those healed to respond in faith with thanksgiving and love as the leper did in Luke 17:15-19, and as the demon-possessed man did in Mark 5:18-20. By God's grace, physical healing should lead to spiritual healing (faith in Jesus) and eternal life with him in heaven.

Those who have this gift are compassionate toward the sick and pray over them regularly. They have great faith and trust that God can and will heal some and are not deterred when he chooses not to. They are motivated knowing that God's revealed power will draw people to faith in Jesus. Their ultimate concern is the spiritual well-being of those being healed and their relationship with Jesus. They yearn for the day when there will be no more pain and suffering, and sin will no longer wreak havoc on the people of God. See 1 Corinthians 12:9, 28, 30, James 5:13-16.

Thoughts – how do I use this gift? How can I use it more? How could I develop it and use it more effectively? What support do I need to ask for?

Spiritual Gift of Leadership

Short Definition
The special ability the Holy Spirit gives to recognise and communicate God's purposes and to accomplish them through the motivation and direction of a group of people.

Extended Definition
The spiritual gift of leadership is closely related to the gift of administration and, interestingly, the spiritual gift of pastor/shepherd. The Greek word for the spiritual gift of leadership is proistemi. This word means to lead, to assist, to protect and to care for others.

The spiritual gift of leadership is found in Romans 12:8 sandwiched between the gifts of giving and of mercy. It is placed there intentionally to show that it is a gift associated with caring for others. This is what connects it to the gift of pastor/shepherd, and what differentiates it from the gift of administration. It is more people-oriented than task-oriented in its application. This is not to say those with the gift of administration do not care for people; of course they do, but those with the spiritual gift of leadership focus on people and relationships more directly.

The word proistemi is connected to caring for people in other passages as well. In 1 Thessalonians 5:12-13 Paul says to 'respect those who labour among you and are over (proistemi) you in the Lord and admonish you, and to esteem them very highly in love because of their work.' The labour and work of those who were leading the believers in Thessalonica was that of tirelessly caring for their souls. Paul also connects leadership to caring for others when he asks, 'If someone does not know how to manage (proistemi) his own household, how will he care for God's church?' 1 Timothy 3:5

The Holy Spirit gives the spiritual gift of leadership to some in the church to care for God's people and lead them into deeper relationship with Christ and each other. They base their success on how well they help others succeed and grow in their spiritual walk with Jesus. They are able to accomplish many different tasks and objectives as they lead, but they will always lead relationally and with a deep concern for the well-being of others. They are 'visionary' and less concerned with mundane details than those with the spiritual gift of administration. Many are entrepreneurial and willing to take risks to see the kingdom of God advanced through the church. They will go to great lengths to protect those under their care and are well-equipped to lead through crisis situations. See also Romans 12:8; 1 Thessalonians 5:12; 1

Timothy 3:4-5, 12; 5:17.

Thoughts – how do I use this gift? How can I use it more? How could I develop it and use it more effectively? What support do I need to ask for?

Using My Gifts – One Year Planner

Use this sheet to help you think about how you are currently using your gifts and then to plan how you can increase your use of them in the future.

Gift Name e.g., administration	
Now How are you using this gift now? E.g., Co-leading a life group, ensuring that structures and planning are organized and working well in advance, being part of the children's ministry team. Now shade the square to indicate what % of your non-sleeping and eating time you are using this gift	
Next What can you do immediately to increase your use of this gift? E.g., Take an increasing role in leading my group. Offer my expertise to other leaders who are looking at things on a day-to-day basis. Take on an increasing coordination role in the children's work.	
Next year If you could not fail, in the next 12 months what will God do with your gift? Dream big! E.g I would be leading a ministry in the discipleship sphere – helping people integrate into the church.	

Using My Gifts – One Year Planner

Use this sheet to help you think about how you are currently using your gifts and then to plan how you can increase your use of them in the future.

Gift Name e.g., administration	
Now How are you using this gift now? E.g., Co-leading a life group, ensuring that structures and planning are organized and working well in advance, being part of the children's ministry team. Now shade the square to indicate what % of your non-sleeping and eating time you are using this gift	
Next What can you do immediately to increase your use of this gift? E.g., Take an increasing role in leading my group. Offer my expertise to other leaders who are looking at things on a day-to-day basis. Take on an increasing coordination role in the children's work.	
Next year If you could not fail, in the next 12 months what will God do with your gift? Dream big! E.g I would be leading a ministry in the discipleship sphere – helping people integrate into the church.	

Using My Gifts – One Year Planner

Use this sheet to help you think about how you are currently using your gifts and then to plan how you can increase your use of them in the future.

Gift Name e.g., administration	
Now How are you using this gift now? E.g., Co-leading a life group, ensuring that structures and planning are organized and working well in advance, being part of the children's ministry team. Now shade the square to indicate what % of your non-sleeping and eating time you are using this gift	
Next What can you do immediately to increase your use of this gift? E.g., Take an increasing role in leading my group. Offer my expertise to other leaders who are looking at things on a day-to-day basis. Take on an increasing coordination role in the children's work.	
Next year If you could not fail, in the next 12 months what will God do with your gift? Dream big! E.g I would be leading a ministry in the discipleship sphere – helping people integrate into the church.	

NOTES

NOTES

BE BOLD STOP FAFFING ABOUT AND CRACK ON FOR JESUS